THE WORLD OF THE POLAR BEAR

The World of the Polar Bear

N O R B E R T   R O S I N G

FIREFLY BOOKS

A Firefly Book

Published by Firefly Books Ltd. 2006

First printing

Publisher Cataloging-in-Publication Data (U.S.)
Rosing, Norbert.
    The world of the polar bear / Norbert Rosing.
[204] p. : col. photos., maps ;   cm.
Includes bibliographical references and index.
Summary: Season-by-season account of the life of polar bears, including hunting, mating, rearing cubs, and journeying to and from the ice.
ISBN-13: 978-1-55407-155-5
ISBN-10: 1-55407-155-0
1. Polar bear. 2. Polar bear—Pictorial works. I. Title.
599.78/6 dc22   QL737.C27.R67 2006

Library and Archives Canada Cataloguing in Publication
Rosing, Norbert
    The world of the polar bear / Norbert Rosing. — 1st ed.
Includes bibliographical references and index.
ISBN-13: 978-1-55407-155-5
ISBN-10: 1-55407-155-0
1. Polar bear. 2. Polar bear—Pictorial works. I. Title.
QL737.C27R664 2006 599.786 C2006-900460-9

Published in the United States by
Firefly Books (U.S.) Inc.
P.O. Box 1338, Ellicott Station
Buffalo, New York 14205

Published in Canada by
Firefly Books Ltd.
66 Leek Crescent
Richmond Hill, Ontario L4B 1H1

Cover and interior design by Sari Naworynski
Scanning and color fidelity by Moveable Inc. (www.moveable.com)

Printed in Singapore

The publisher gratefully acknowledges the financial support for our publishing program by the Canada Council for the Arts, the Ontario Arts Council and the Government of Canada through the Book Publishing Industry Development Program.

AUTHOR'S NOTE

The photographs in this book have not been digitally altered. What you see here is exactly what the photographer captured on film.

Readers interested in purchasing any of the images in this book should contact National Geographic Image Collection at www.ngsimages.com, or the photographer at www.rosing.de.

CONTENTS

Above: Mothers with single cubs are always being pestered by their playful three-month-olds. On this windy, bitterly cold day this mother's head was a convenient resting place for her cub. Bears always lie with their backs to the wind, so I was forced to face into it. With a temperature of –18° F (–28° C), by the end of the day the batteries on four cameras had failed and my fingertips and face were frostbitten, but the results were well worth it.

Right: Mother and cub enjoy their first days in the sun, gently playing, mouthing and wrestling with each other.

FOREWORD

So long as the human ear can hark back to the breaking of waves over deep seas; so long as the human eye can follow the gleam of the Northern Lights over the silent snow fields; then so long, no doubt, will the lure of the unknown draw restless souls into those great Arctic wastes.

— Polar explorer Roald Amundsen, *Our Polar Flight* (1925)

Living in the Arctic is an experience most of us will never have. Summers are filled with endless days when the tundra is alive with multicolored flowers and wild berries. The swarms of mosquitoes are so fierce that even the caribou move to the coast in search of a gentle breeze. In winter the endless darkness is interrupted only by the occasional fireworks show known as the aurora borealis.

We are lucky to have Norbert Rosing as our guide in this journey of discovery to the northernmost part of the world. Through his sensitive photography we discover that those legendary vast spaces of the Arctic are full of wonder, drama and tenderness. Norbert is not content with just documenting the existence of exotic wildlife in unusual locations. His gift as a photographer is his great curiosity about the natural world. His magic is displayed in photographs that weave light, color and action into a tapestry that tells volumes about life in the Far North.

In this wonderful book we accompany Norbert to some of the world's remotest regions, where we meet the polar bear up close and personal. Not only do we witness snarling encounters between males, but we also observe a mother as she patiently endures the constant ear pulling of her playful cubs. Norbert's love for the North is rivaled only by his love of the polar bear and of photography. No photographer has been able to understand the complexities of the life cycle of the polar bear and to bring them to life in such an evocative way as Norbert

Rosing. His intuitiveness and perseverance have led him to explore a polar bear den, as well as to follow the animal across frozen seas with its companion, the elusive and enchanting arctic fox.

As we turn the pages of *The World of the Polar Bear*, we realize that the vastness of the tundra we are so used to hearing about is full of excitement and danger. The polar bear is not alone in its fight for survival in this harsh environment. Muskoxen stand in a circle protecting their young from possible predators. As spring approaches, a walrus calf on an ice floe suckles contentedly as its mother keeps a watchful eye on a nearby polar bear and her cubs. We can almost hear the roar of a herd of walrus plunging into the water in unison when a curious and hungry bear approaches.

On long winter nights the northern lights add even more drama to the spectacle of wildlife and scenery in the Arctic. This book once again capitalizes on Norbert's poetic talents by showing the intricate shapes and patterns of the aurora borealis and other weather-related phenomena.

The adventure part of this book is a must-read for anyone interested in surviving adverse conditions in less than favorable weather. As Norbert's editor at *National Geographic Magazine*, I have found myself editing photographs of his quests and admonishing him, "Norbert, don't ever do this again." There is usually silence at the other end of the transatlantic call, then he responds with a chuckle, "It wasn't as bad as it looks." Indeed, Norbert has risked his life in order to bring us the extraordinary pictures contained in this book.

Someone once said that life is not measured by the number of breaths we take, but by the moments that take our breath away. In *The World of the Polar Bear* Norbert Rosing shows us how to live life to its fullest.

John A. Echave, Senior Editor, *National Geographic Magazine*

This mother was resting on the tundra, her cub playing on her back, when she suddenly decided to stand up. The baby didn't want to let go and seemed to be enjoying the view. I have often seen mother bears carry their offspring on their backs, but only for short distances.

PREFACE

My arctic adventure began in a Winnipeg library late one February afternoon in 1983. Just a few hours earlier, I had stepped off a bus from Montreal. I had intended to spend the night in Manitoba's capital before continuing west to the Yukon. My plans, however, were about to change dramatically.

Stooped over the library's maps of the Canadian North, I was anticipating the trip ahead when I was interrupted by a young Inuk. "Planning a trip north?" he asked. When I nodded, he continued, "The arctic experience in winter is mostly about learning to love the cold. Luckily, you don't have to go all the way to Resolute Bay to find it. Just take the train north to Churchill." He pointed to a dot on the shore of Hudson Bay. "If it isn't cold enough for you there, I'd recommend a trip to the South Pole."

Intrigued, I took his advice and boarded the train for Churchill the next morning. After a 36-hour trip through wheat fields followed by what seemed like endless boreal forest, we reached our destination. A sudden storm had transformed the town into an icy desert. Like a tortoise in its shell, I retreated deep into my parka, hoisted my heavy knapsack over my shoulder and fought my way towards the town's only open hotel.

The next two days were spoiled by my inexperience with the Arctic. I saw a dazzling display of northern lights, but my film froze in the bitterly cold temperatures and my camera stopped working altogether. I phoned my folks in Germany, but even their familiar voices couldn't alleviate my sense of disappointment and frustration. Fleeing on a plane, I had no idea that Churchill and the Far North would one day become my home away from home.

Before the early 1980s, not many people were familiar with Churchill, aside from the prairie wheat farmers who shipped their grain to Canada's only arctic seaport, and employees of Canadian National Railways who rode the desolate lines to this northern terminus. Seven hundred miles by air from Winnipeg, the town is at a latitude of 58 degrees 44 minutes north, the same as Stockholm, Sweden, and Oslo, Norway. The view of the town from an airplane perfectly reveals its isolation, right in the middle of the tundra that skirts the true Arctic.

In the past two decades, Churchill has become an internationally renowned center for wildlife research and ecotourism, its name synonymous with polar bears, northern lights, massive bird migrations, whale pods and a harsh landscape that surprises visitors by yielding colorful annual crops of wildflowers. Scientists, photographers and film teams are among the thousands of people who flock to the town each year.

In the five years following my first visit to Churchill, the aurora borealis display stayed in my mind, and I returned in March 1988 to try again to capture it on film. It proved to be one of the best years ever for this spectacular phenomenon, and I couldn't contain my enthusiasm. People in town took note and kindly offered advice on other subjects I might want to photograph: the snow goose migration, the ice breakup, the beluga whales, the wildflowers and, of course, the polar bears.

Since those first visits to the Far North, I have evolved from a novice hobbyist into a professional photographer. "Up there," hours of total frustration mixed with moments of pure happiness are part of any photographer's life. Sitting in tents waiting out storms, dealing with broken equipment and being at the wrong place at the wrong time can make life miserable. But capturing a polar bear mother interacting with her cubs or traveling through a pristine wonderland under cloudless skies more than makes up for the bad times. Working with experienced guides and wildlife experts, not to mention cultivating patience, has been the key to any success I have had as a photographer. To capture a moment in the wild takes 1/250 of a second; to find the right place at the right time in the right light and with the right equipment can take weeks, even years in the case of some shots.

Over the past 17 years, I have returned to the Churchill area at least twice a year. Today my wife, Elli, and I are proud to be welcomed back as semipermanent residents. I have also had the opportunity to travel farther north – to photograph arctic foxes and muskoxen on Victoria Island, walrus at Coral Harbour and Igloolik, beluga whales off Somerset Island and narwhal off Baffin Island. But the polar bear, ever since I first saw one swimming in a northern lake, has become my primary subject. From that first contact I experienced a rush of adrenaline, a heady hybrid of respect and awe that has continued to fuel my passion for *Ursus maritimus* and the northern land it inhabits.

Like any other fever, the polar bear bug has a number of symptoms, not the least of which is simple admiration for the bears. Its lingering effect also includes a deep appreciation for all northern regions, where your mind is free to roam across a vast landscape. It awakens your senses to the richness inherent in this austere land, where the clean, crisp air can be fractured by the haunting calls of cranes, loons and wild geese flying overhead or by the unrelenting whir of a mosquito buzzing about your head.

This is a land that demands respect. Yet, despite its remoteness and size and apparent strength, the Far North is fragile. Climate change, oil and mineral exploration, overhunting – all create effects that ripple through an intricately balanced and interconnected natural world.

Just a short time ago I again began to concentrate on photographing in the Hudson Bay–James Bay Lowlands. Even after all my years there I still discover "white spots" on the map, places I have never been. One of these was Wapusk, a national park southeast of Churchill. Polar bears den in the park, giving birth to a new generation in what is now a protected area. I hope this book will inspire you to support the work of the tireless people who are striving to safeguard the polar bear and its irreplaceable world.

INTRODUCTION

Wapusk National Park is synonymous with polar bears, its name being the local Cree word for "white bear." Before you turn to Norbert's spectacular photographs, allow me in a few short paragraphs to connect the bears with the land.

The park, which was established in 1996, represents the Hudson Bay–James Bay Lowlands natural region, an exciting addition to Canada's world-renowned system of national parks. The lands chosen for the park are significant nationally and internationally for their biological diversity, for their importance as habitat for migrating and breeding birds, and for polar bears. Wapusk, like all of Canada's national parks, not only protects the land and its ecosystems for future generations but is also a place for us to experience, enjoy and share.

The park begins at the western shores of Hudson Bay, transforming from ocean and tidal flats across ancient beach ridges and marshes, through the unending ponds and streams of the peatlands, to the stunted spruce forest where taiga meets tundra. This is the southern edge of the Arctic, a region symbolized by the polar bear.

A complex relationship of ice, climate, ocean currents, habitat and the biological drive to survive creates a concentration of polar bears in Wapusk National Park. Polar bears spend most of their time on the sea ice. The ice on Hudson Bay melts completely every year, forcing the bears onto the land. As the ice breaks up, currents in the bay bring it south, depositing most of the western Hudson Bay population of bears in Wapusk. On land, most of the bears stay on or near the shore waiting for the bay to freeze again. But the pregnant females have another objective. They move inland to the central and western part of Wapusk, where there is an abundance of suitable habitat for maternity dens. There the female will give birth to her cubs and care for them in the den until late in the winter, when they are able to travel with her back to the ice and prey on Hudson Bay.

The concentration of dens in the park is due to the area's abundance of suitable denning habitat. These polar bears dig dens in the earth rather than completely in snow, and a suitable den site has strict requirements: It must drift over with snow, providing insulation and a space to enlarge the den; the soil must be free of rocks and other obstructions; and the roof must be supported to prevent collapse. The ponds and creeks cut into the peatlands, and their fringes of stunted spruce provide ideal locations. The peat bank faces are several meters high and nearly vertical. The mat of spruce roots near the ground provides stability for the den's roof. The trunks and branches and the southeast banks catch the snow blown by the prevailing northwest winter winds, creating large, firm drifts. In short, an ideal spot for a den.

Parks Canada's primary objective in managing a national park is maintaining ecological integrity. For polar bears this means protecting their habitats from development and change. It means making sure that the bears are not disturbed unnecessarily. Our mandate is to ensure that Canadians have an opportunity to see these magnificent animals in their native surroundings. We are also guides, opening our places of discovery and learning to visitors from around the world. This book is an opportunity to glimpse polar bears and their world, both in Wapusk National Park and elsewhere in Canada.

— Campbell Elliott, Superintendent, Wapusk National Park

A winter storm was forecast for the western Hudson Bay area. In the morning I drove out of Churchill and caught sight of a bear resting in a snowdrift. Within minutes the storm hit. In the whiteout the bear lifted its head above the drift's rim and watched as I took its picture. Then I slowly made my way back to town.

This is the only time I have ever seen polar bears wrestling on a lake in a snowstorm. The visibility was down to less than 55 yards (50 meters) and the background disappeared in the white whirl of snowflakes and ice crystals.

Polar bears are the largest land carnivores in the world. The largest male ever recorded near Churchill weighed more than 1,540 pounds (700 kilograms). To watch these mammoth animals play-fight is to witness one of the most awe-inspiring spectacles in nature.

SPRING

In the south, tangible signs of spring appear during the month of May. But in the Hudson Bay–James Bay Lowlands, well into the middle of the same month, the temperature barely nudges above freezing and, on a typical day, bitter cold winds still send threatening snow clouds sailing across the sky.

On rare occasions, though, you can enjoy a glimpse of brighter days to come. The cloud cover parts briefly and the sun floods the land with new energy. Arctic animals are starved for light after long, bitterly cold nights. Year-long residents sheltering beneath the snow – the lemming in its pukak *tunnel and the polar bear family in its den – emerge eagerly into the sunlight. All manner of migrants from the south begin to arrive daily by air, sea and land to take part in the short warm season, a season of birth and constant change.*

When the winds finally shift and the all-too-familiar northerly gusts have changed to lilting southerly breezes, they carry with them the faint sounds of distant honking. It is the seasonal migration of the snow geese, and their annual air show heralds the arrival of spring in the North.

THE POLAR BEAR'S DEN

The countryside whizzed past beneath us in a green-and-white patchwork stitched together from the alternating fabrics of conifers and snow. Heading south, we crossed the tree line and followed the route of a meandering creek, where we noticed large snowdrifts deposited on the lee side, an ideal location for polar bear dens. When the helicopter pilot suddenly spied bear tracks directly below, he executed a steep descending turn that gave me a momentary flashback to my morning meal.

Flying close to the tops of the highest trees near the creek, we were able to follow the tracks. "There she is," I heard Dennis Andriashek, a Canadian Wildlife Service scientist, shout through the earphones. "She's sticking her head out of the den. And look! There's a young one." As we banked to the right I was struck at once by how elusive these maternal groups are, even in the most heavily populated denning habitat in the country.

In recent years I have searched for polar bear families with the help of Morris and Mike Spence, and their friend Allen (Amak) Oman. The Spence brothers not only own the famous Wat'chee Lodge, located on the edge of Wapusk National Park, but they also serve as guides to tourists, photographers and film teams visiting the area. It's not an easy task to find the dens, given how well camouflaged they are and the size of the park. I once asked Morris what his secret was.

"There is no secret," he replied. "This is all tribal land. Everything I learned out there I learned from my father, other family members and friends. I can read the clouds for weather changes, the color of the ice, the snowdrifts. I travel with open eyes and an open mind and try to put myself in a polar bear mother's position searching for shelter."

In anticipation of the arrival of their offspring, the Wapusk female bears dig earth dens or move into existing ones used over the years by many generations. Females in other denning areas search for a suitable snowdrift in which to excavate a comfortable chamber. They usually dig out a single room averaging 6 by 10 feet (2 by 3 meters) in area and 4 feet (1.2 meters) high, but two- and even three-room dens are not uncommon. The den's roof is thin enough to allow oxygen to pass through the snow crystals – so thin, in fact, that a fellow photographer once strolled over a slope and broke through one. Fortunately, his leg plunged into an unoccupied spare room!

In her *igloovikus*, as the Inuit call it, the bear drifts in and out of sleep, living off her fat stores from the previous winter's hunting and waiting to give birth. The young are born sometime between November and December. Twins and, less frequently, triplets make up the typical polar bear family; only one litter of four has ever been documented.

At birth, the polar bear cub is smaller than a tree squirrel, weighing less than 2 pounds (1 kilogram). With only a light down covering and its eyes still sealed shut, the newborn is completely helpless. In this undeveloped condition the cubs are vulnerable to the cold. Scientists have found that the mother's body heat coupled with the insulating layers of snow covering the den can keep the inside temperatures

A mother bear's claw marks are still visible on the walls of this *igloovikus*.

only a few degrees below freezing, regardless of how frigid the outside temperatures become. During their first three weeks of life, the cubs curl up on their mother's thighs for protection from the frozen ground.

Helpless though they may be during these early weeks, newborn cubs are equipped with long, sharp claws that enable them to comb through their mother's thick fur to reach her nipples. Polar bears produce the fattiest milk among bears – about 40 percent – which helps the cubs grow quickly. After just one month on this high-fat diet, the cubs begin to crawl. At six weeks of age they are able to open their eyes fully, and at ten weeks, when they weigh about 25 pounds (11 kilograms)

and can keep their balance, they are ready to venture outside the den.

Around this time, as the days start to get longer and warmer, the mother crawls outside to stretch her limbs. Her coat is soiled from the long months in the den and spangled with balls of frosted ice. After a few solo outings she entices her chubby, reluctant cubs to follow her out into the world, where they will enter their first – and most critical – season of life. At first they stick close to their parent, but then they begin to play, which helps them grow stronger and develop their coordination in the snow. Initially the cubs restrict their play to the vicinity of the den in case danger or bad weather demands a hasty retreat. But acclimatiza-

This snow den and its three entrances may have been dug by a mother looking for cleaner accommodation after three months in her nearby earth den.

tion to the winter environment is part of arctic life, and the quicker the cubs adapt, the better their long-term chances for survival.

On one occasion we found a freshly dug snow den about 55 yards (50 meters) from a deep earth den. At the entrance to the earth den we could still see hoarfrost from the breath of the bear family. Morris speculates that after three months the mother was tired of the old den and wanted cleaner, brighter accommodation. She found a long snowdrift facing south with a good view over the surrounding landscape, and hollowed out a new den in the middle of it. Her long claw strokes around the den and the small paw prints of her twins were still visible in the snow.

After a week or two close to home, mother and babies start their long walk to Hudson Bay. Inuit call this journey *ah-tik-tok* ("those who wander to the sea").

For me this time with the new families is always inspiring. What better way to celebrate the arrival of spring than witnessing the arrival of a new polar bear family?

Above: A mother and cub peek out of a day den dug for protection from bad weather. A bitterly cold day with strong winds had kept the bears inside until late afternoon, when they appeared at the den's entrance for only a few seconds.

Right: This was a momentous day for me – the first time I had ever seen a mother bear and her cub leaving their den after the winter. The mother is rolling in the snow to clean herself while the cub is still not ready to come out.

These playful twins and triplets are about three months old and perhaps a week out of their den. During their first week of exploration, cubs rarely stray far from their mother. When they do, she quickly calls them to her side using a noisy puffing sound, called chuffing.

 These photographs were taken on cloudy days with a long telephoto lens. The diffused lighting eliminates sharp contrasts and in this case allowed me to use the branches of the dwarf tamarack and willows as a surprisingly soft backdrop for the families.

Mothers play with their cubs for a long time – several hours – before settling down for a nap with their cubs on their back.

JOURNEY TO THE ICE

The Wapusk denning area is located about 10 to 40 miles (16 to 65 kilometers) from the Hudson Bay coastline. Walking all that way is a hardship for a nursing mother, particularly one that has been fasting for eight months. Nevertheless, she sets out at a steady pace, once in a while rescuing a straggler and always allowing adequate time for her offspring to nurse, rest and play. A low growl or a light cuff brings any misbehaving cub quickly into line. After three or four days of traversing frozen ponds and negotiating ditches filled with fresh powdered snow, the family will reach the shore of the ice-covered bay.

Conveniently, the polar bear's favorite prey gives birth on the ice in the early spring. Like all seals, the female ringed seal produces a single pup. And, much like the polar bear, she cares for her young in a hollowed-out den in a snowdrift or a natural snow cave covering one of her breathing holes. The den provides protection from the weather, but not from a hungry polar bear. Its acute sense of smell can easily detect a seal's lair. The immobile seal pups weigh about 10 pounds (4.5 kilograms) at birth but quickly double their birth weight, and 75 percent of their nutritional content is available to the polar bear as high-calorie fat.

Polar bear courtship and mating also take place on the sea ice during April and May. Female polar bears are known as induced ovulators, which means that they don't ovulate regularly but rely instead on the mating ritual to stimulate ovulation. To ensure that mating is successful, partners may stay together for an entire week. The birth of thousands of seal pups in the spring provides ideal fare for newly expectant female bears, which must increase their weight as much as possible to survive the months ahead.

As the polar bear family sets out across the ice, the mother immediately starts to hunt for her first feast of seal after her long fast. Although the ringed seal is their primary source of food, polar bears also hunt bearded seals, hooded seals, harp seals and harbor seals. At this time of year the bears eat only the high-calorie skin and fat. They leave the rest of the carcass for arctic foxes, ravens and other northern scavengers.

The mother keeps a constant watch over her family. Adult male bears, which stand to increase their own reproductive success by eliminating unrelated cubs, pose the greatest risk. On the feeding grounds the mother tries to protect her cubs by hunting in secluded areas, away from other bears.

Occasionally wolves pose a threat as well. Morris and Amak once watched as a black wolf approached a mother and her cub. When it came within 40 feet (12 meters) of the two, the mother became nervous and began hissing and snorting while waving her head from side to side. When that didn't work, she charged the wolf. It ran several yards away, stopped and headed back towards the cub – the bear charged again. After repeating the exercise once more, the wolf gave up. A pack has a better chance of success than a single wolf; several wolves will keep the mother busy while other members of the pack attack the young.

At the end of their first day on the ice, the mother digs a pit in the snow where she can nurse the cubs and sleep protected from the wind.

Chapter Two

A cub tries and fails to
follow its mother up a
steep snowbank. After
a few minutes its calls
for help bring mother
to the rescue.

A strong wind doesn't prevent napping and playtime on the open tundra.

Cubs nurse for at least 20 months, growing quickly on their mother's rich milk. I took these photographs just before scientists began examining the tranquilized mother bear.

Above: Polar bear families prefer to move into stands of trees for shelter before they start nursing or resting. Larch and spruce trees provide a windscreen for this mother and cub on a gray, windy day.

Right: Cute scenes like this "give me five" photo are a reward for long hours spent waiting in the cold.

Although ringed seals are the polar bear's primary prey, harp seals and their pups are an important food source for the Davis Strait polar bear population north of Labrador.

Above: To keep the breathing hole open, a harp seal mother uses her claws to widen the opening in the ice. Seal pups on the ice provide little challenge for a hungry bear, but catching a surfacing seal at its breathing hole requires skill and patience.

Left: A harp seal pup wakes up after a snowstorm. Only 10 to 14 days after birth, pups weigh approximately 90 pounds (40 kilograms). Scientists have found that the polar bear's diet of seal pups in the spring can provide most of its yearly calorie intake.

ARCTIC SPRING

One April evening in the central Arctic I had cause to envy the bear families tucked in for the night. A snowdrift was forming against the side of the tent and the temperature had dropped to 1.4° F (–17° C). The warmth of spring seemed a very distant memory. It didn't help that my guide and I were lost, not to mention cold, hungry and thirsty. Somewhere out there in the blowing snow lay our destination: Cambridge Bay, a hamlet on the southeast coast of Victoria Island.

While Wapusk National Park is located near the southernmost limit of the polar bear's range in Hudson Bay, Victoria Island lies north of the Arctic Circle, straddling the Northwest Territories and Nunavut. Its polar bear population shares the immense island of rolling hills, lakes and rocky tundra with caribou, wolves, fox, arctic hare and muskoxen. It was the bison-like muskoxen that I had come to see.

The day began with fine, sunny weather. I had received word that a herd had been sighted near Mount Pelly, a large hill not far from Cambridge Bay. One of the town's young residents offered to go with me, and since it was going to take just a few hours to travel there and back on snowmobiles, we set off with what we had with us: a komatik sled for our gear, one small tent, a sleeping bag, a leftover sandwich from lunch, a can of ginger ale and a chocolate bar. As we were about to leave, one of my guide's friends handed him a GPS (global positioning system) receiver. Neither of us knew how to use it, but it was a sunny afternoon, so we didn't give it much thought.

We headed northeast towards Mount Pelly. After about two hours,

we still hadn't sighted the muskoxen – and we never would. A gray wall of cloud moved in and we suddenly found ourselves in a blizzard. Arctic weather can be very unpredictable – sunny and dead calm one moment and whiteout conditions with high winds the next. We turned around and drove in what we hoped was the right direction, but the visibility was poor. After a few miles the guide admitted that he had no idea where we were. Time to pull out the GPS: The reading seemed to indicate that we were about 11 miles (18 kilometers) from town. We set off again into the storm.

By the time the sun was setting – around 11 p.m. – ice crystals had formed around my mouth and nose and my snowmobile was starting to act up. We checked the distance again and discovered that we were still 11 miles from Cambridge Bay. Something wasn't right. Ordinarily, you would simply follow the arrow on the GPS screen and arrive at your destination. What we didn't know was that to get an exact reading you have to be moving, either walking or driving. Instead we had stopped several times to take readings and then crisscrossed the tundra, losing precious time and fuel.

At midnight, with both machines low on gas, we decided to pitch the tent, using the snowmobiles and komatik as anchors to keep our flimsy shelter from blowing away. We shared the chocolate bar – the sandwich had been eaten earlier in the day – but the pop was frozen. Nothing to eat and nothing to drink. I couldn't believe how careless we had been. How could we have gone out into this harsh land without the

basics for survival? I blamed myself. Like many of his generation, my young friend no doubt thought he was invincible. I was old enough to know better.

After a cold, restless night we crawled out of the tent, hoping the wind had died down. It hadn't, but there was enough visibility to see a short distance, so we set off again. After a few miles my companion stopped his machine without any warning and turned to me with a big grin. "Here's an old trail!" he shouted. "It should take us back to town." I wanted to believe him, and when my snowmobile broke down and he had to drag me along in his komatik, I desperately wanted to believe him. Thankfully, he was right. We arrived back in town to the great relief of everyone, including the search party that had been sent out to look for us. Since that harrowing experience I never travel in the Arctic without an experienced Inuk guide, a GPS – which I now know how to work – a satellite phone and survival gear.

It is impossible to go through such an experience without gaining an appreciation for the unique characteristics and survival skills of the animals that make their home in the High Arctic. The muskox, which I returned to photograph another day, is a perfect example. This distant relative of sheep and goats boasts a number of physical adaptations that allow it to survive in the Far North. Its qiviut, a woolly layer that lies beneath its shaggy coat, is eight times warmer than sheep's wool, while the muskox's rounded hooves allow it to walk through soft snow without sinking and to dig through the snow to reach the grasses, sedges and willows below. Even the calves, which are born in the spring, emerge into their frosty world wearing wool coats.

Above: At midnight toward the end of May, a Victoria Island herd of muskoxen is framed by sundogs. The majority of Canada's approximately 85,000 muskoxen are found on Victoria Island, Banks Island and the other islands of the arctic archipelago. The only other naturally occurring population lives in Greenland.

Left: Hoarfrost covers low-lying vegetation on Victoria Island. A longer view, from a hilltop west of Cambridge Bay in mid-May, appears on page 52.

A group of male and female muskoxen face into a strong wind. If threatened, muskoxen form a protective ring, the calves running quickly to their mothers' sides. The calves, which are born between April and June, are able to walk within hours of birth and already wear the thick coat that inspired the muskox's Inuit name, *omingmak*, "the animal with skin like a beard."

SUMMER

◆ ◆ ◆ ◆ ◆ ◆ ◆ ◆ ◆

Kerchhoffer Falls on Southampton Island.

By mid-June the gradual changes of spring in the North – the white winter coats of the fox and hare changing to brown, the hours of daylight lengthening, the temperatures rising – give way to the explosive transformations of summer. Loons and swans search for food on lakes that were frozen just a few days before. Seemingly overnight, summer wildflowers in riotous, unexpected colors brighten the harsh ground. And the soft summer air is filled with the chirps, calls and buzzing of thousands of insects and birds, punctuated with the tiny pops of air bubbles being released from the melting ice.

In the newly ice-free coastal waters of Hudson Bay, pods of beluga whales appear. Dense herds of these sociable animals gather at the mouths of the Seal and Churchill rivers, where some use the rocky shallows and sand bars to shed their old skin, wildly thrashing their tail fins and occasionally stretching their heads above the surface.

On the Barrens the muskoxen shed their winter fur, the discarded quiviut flying over the tundra like cotton grass. Polar bears also moult during the summer months, and with the breakup of the ice on their offshore hunting grounds, they are on the move.

ICE BREAKUP

Two of the most vital feeding sites for polar bears foraging on the pack ice are areas of open water known as leads and polynyas. Leads are ice-free stretches of water that follow the coastline in linear fashion and teem with arctic wildlife. The entire perimeter of Hudson Bay, for example, is outlined by a lead created by strong winds, currents and tidal motions, while a similar and much larger system completely encircles the polar basin in the High Arctic. Russian explorer and biologist Savva Uspenskii named the latter system the "arctic ring of life" because of its significance in the cycle of polar ecosystems. Polynyas, on the other hand, are irregularly shaped arctic ponds that range in size from a few hundred square yards to hundreds of square miles.

The same tidal forces that keep polynyas and leads free of ice also stir up the rich organic nutrients from the water column that support plankton, the building block of the pelagic (open sea) food chain. As a result, these areas are critical for the survival of many arctic species. Birds rely on leads and polynyas early in their breeding season, when no other sources of food are available. Marine mammals such as seals and walruses, which need access to both water and air, can always be spotted nearby. It is little wonder that these hotbeds of wildlife activity, which are located in roughly the same area year after year, are popular among hungry polar bears.

When the arctic ice begins to melt at the beginning of summer, some polar bear populations follow the receding ice north to hunt. They capture seals by stalking – sneaking up on their prey as it lies on the ice by its breathing hole and then charging it – or, more commonly, by still-hunting – waiting motionless by the breathing hole until the seal surfaces and then killing it and lifting it out of the water with one blow of a massive paw. Another hunting technique is what polar bear expert Dr. Ian Stirling calls the "aquatic stalk." As marine mammals, polar bears are accomplished swimmers, and they will sometimes stalk seals, or even ducks and sea birds, in stretches of open water.

In areas where the sea ice melts in the summer, the bears are forced to come ashore. By June and July the breakup in Hudson Bay has begun, and free-floating ice sheets with bears on board drift south to James Bay. The bears stay on the massive icy rafts as long as possible, until the melting of the ice sheets forces them to swim ashore. Facing a long wait until the next winter, they begin to live largely off their fat reserves. By mid- to late June, when the bears leave the ice, females have often tripled or quadrupled their weight. This substantial weight increase is essential, particularly for the survival of pregnant females, which have a lengthy stay in the maternity den ahead of them.

Once ashore for the season, the bears sleep or lounge during the day. To conserve energy during this period of "walking hibernation," they often rest in beds dug into the cool earth to escape from the legions of parasitic insects that swarm throughout the North during summer. In these lean times the bears of the Hudson Bay–James Bay Lowlands exploit a diverse range of prey, from mice, gophers, lemmings, bird eggs and nestlings to seal and beluga carcasses that wash ashore. In August and September summer berries are a readily available main-course item for the hungry bears as they wait to be able to return to their hunting grounds on the ice.

Chapter Four

Left: In June a small waterfall runs down an ice wall by the shore of Hudson Bay.

A majestic iceberg is stranded on a huge rock in Eclipse Sound, near Pond Inlet, Baffin Island.

One of the few places to see polar bears in summer is at Sila Lodge, located on Wager Bay, which stretches west off Roes Welcome Sound not far south of the Arctic Circle.

Arctic waters are often close to freezing, even in the summer. When a bear climbs up on an ice floe (left), it shakes the water from its fur to prevent ice from forming on it.

Above: A bear beneath the surface of the water uses its front paws as oars to propel itself through the water and its hind feet as rudders to steer.

Left: To capture this image of a diving bear I used a long pole camera borrowed from the National Geographic Society. A cable that ran from the camera's viewfinder to a pair of video goggles allowed me to see what the camera was seeing.

Following page: In July the sun rises over the last pieces of ice melting in Hudson Bay.

Above: A male arctic tern offers his mate a fish as a courtship gift.

Left: The arctic tern (above) and the Ross's gull (below) are among the many birds that breed in the Arctic. The arctic tern travels the farthest – a 22,000-mile (35,200 km) round-trip from Antarctica.

A bear scatters a flock of fellow scavengers on its way to a whale carcass that has washed up on the shore, a welcome meal in the summer, when food is scarce.

In July beluga whales gather in Cunningham Inlet on Somerset Island in the central Canadian Arctic. They drift into the river with the incoming tides to mate and give birth. The view from an airplane of this amazing congregation of whales is truly breathtaking.

Left: A beluga whale lifts its head out of the water.

Above: In this aerial photograph of belugas, several gray new-borns are visible next to their mothers.

Below: Two bowhead whales surface in Foxe Basin in mid-June. Bowhead whales are endangered in Canadian waters.

Above: Purple saxifrage is the first wildflower to bloom on the tundra
in the spring. "Pillows" of them can be found everywhere beginning in
mid-June.

Right: Large-flowered wintergreen, which blooms in late June and early
July, is one of my favorite arctic flowers.

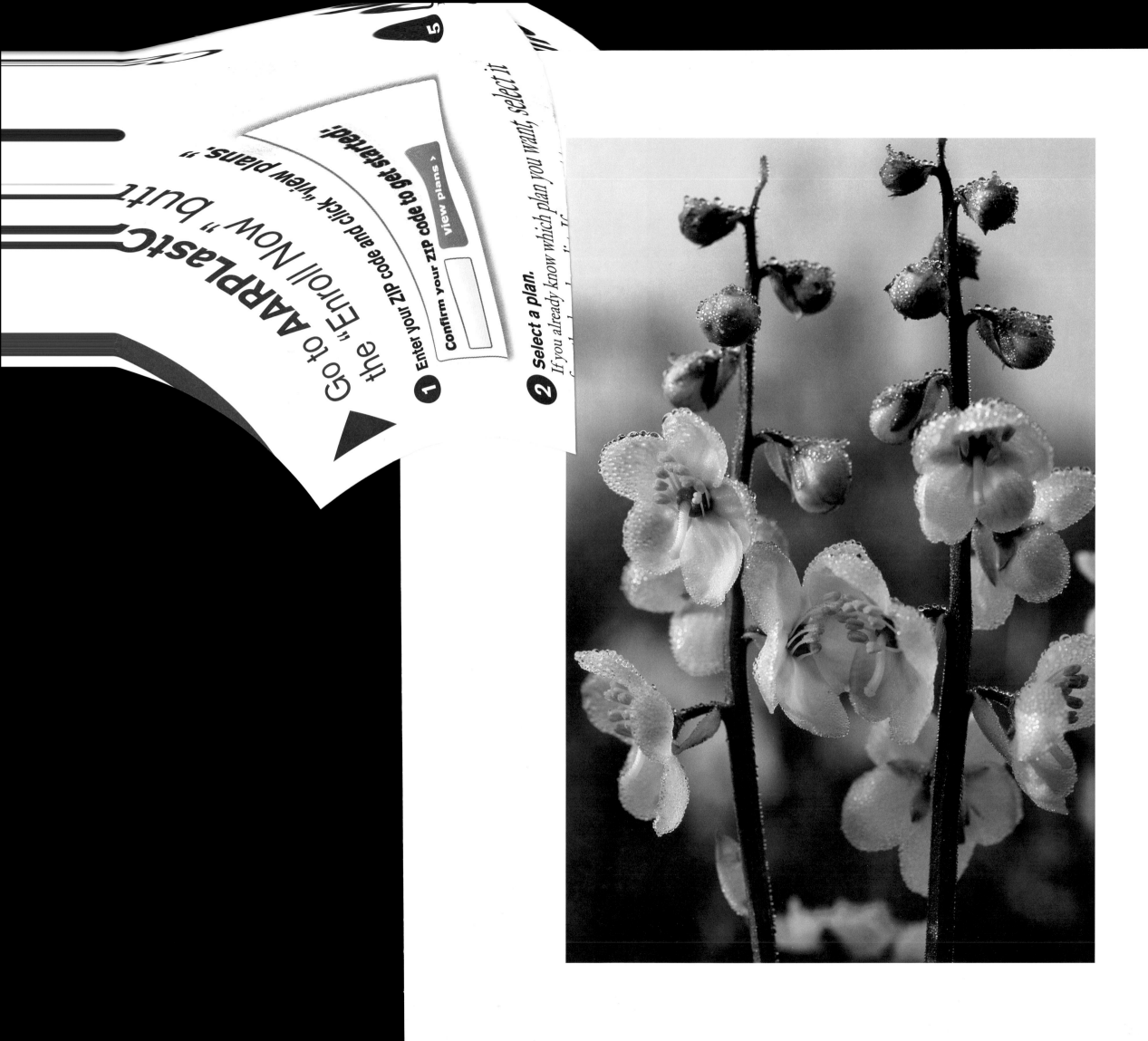

Go to **AARPLastC** the "Enroll Now" butt

► Go to **AARPLastC** the "Enroll Now" butt

1 Enter your ZIP code to get started:

Confirm your ZIP code and click "View plans."

view plans ›

2 Select a plan.
If you already know which plan you want, select it

At the beginning of July, visitors to the Hudson Bay–James Bay Lowlands are often surprised to find rhododendrons such as the Lapland rosebay (above) and orchids such as the round-leaved orchid (below).

Right: A bear rests under a piece of driftwood in the grassy dunes along the Wapusk National Park coastline.

SEARCHING FOR THE ARCTIC FOX

Like the polar bear, the arctic fox is a signature species of the Arctic. Because *Alopex lagopus* is such a superb example of an animal adapted to the arctic habitat, I always look forward to observing it in its natural surroundings.

Opportunistic in their feeding habits, these scavengers search the sea ice for food, taking advantage of the abundant meat from kills left behind by hunting polar bears. Some foxes have been found drifting along on ice floes 125 miles (200 kilometers) from the coast. In May, however, the foxes leave the ice and the pregnant female starts to search for a suitable location in which to give birth to her litter. She excavates a modest den with a few simple entrances and exits. Later in the summer, after the sun has melted the lingering snow and the upper layers of permafrost, the vixen expands her family flat by digging additional exits. Some fox dens are modified to include dozens of entrances and are used by generations of foxes over many decades.

The summer is a perfect time to visit fox dens, when they should be busy with frolicking, photogenic young kits. In June 2003 I flew to Holman, on Victoria Island, to do just that, but when I met my guide, Morris Nigijok, he shook his head. "You haven't picked a very good year for it," he said. "There are hardly any lemmings and geese around."

The population cycles of small rodents and birds are the main factor affecting litter size. The foxes' fecundity waxes and wanes with the food supply available during the spring and summer; they produce as few as five young in some seasons and as many as 25 in others. As often as five times a day the parents bring fresh prey to feed the hungry youngsters. Researchers have counted up to 4,000 lemmings on the menu of a single fox family during the breeding season.

Despite his reservations, Morris agreed to take me out. The snow was melting almost faster than we could find routes for our snowmobiles, so we switched to ATVs and encountered the opposite problem. We were forced to stay as much as possible on what the island's residents call "Eskimo highways": unpaved gravel roads or trails running across the tundra. Over the next several days, the meltwater turned the rolling hills into quagmires of thick, soft clay, perfect for trapping the wheels of even ATVs, which we took turns pulling out of the muck with ropes.

By the last days of June Morris and I had found more than 20 den sites, but none of them were occupied. I was becoming increasingly anxious. This was the time when the young pups emerged from their dens, and I didn't want to miss it. Finally, after many days of being shaken senseless riding around the tundra, Morris found what we were looking for. A small hump sprinkled with mountain avens stood in the middle of an open plain, and seven arctic fox pups were playing nearby. It was the second of July.

For the next six weeks my wife, Elli, and I made our home in a tent pitched 400 yards (365 meters) from the den. Young foxes are born with a velvety covering of dark brown or gray fur. Helpless, naked and blind at birth, they develop quickly and are ready for independence in six months. This litter had already passed the two- or three-week mark.

They were eating solid food and venturing outside, where they played with abandon, yipping and snorting at each other with open mouths.

The following year, the cycle of scarcity and plenty had changed again. Food was plentiful, and friends and I found a den site near Churchill with 13 pups. Filling all those empty little stomachs is a lot of work, and a fox's hunting trips last anywhere from half an hour to several hours. When a vixen delivers a large number of pups, an older daughter from an earlier litter sometimes helps with finding food. However, in the family Elli and I were observing we saw a more familiar helper: the male. Foxes are thought to be monogamous, and both parents are attentive to the young during these early weeks of life. The parents made at least five trips a day, bringing home either lemmings or other voles, ducks, and Canada or snow goose chicks. One day they even brought the leg of a sandhill crane.

At eight weeks of age the kits are old enough to follow their parents on hunting expeditions. By the fall, though, when geese and other migratory birds head south, the mother finds it difficult to keep up with the dietary demands of her young, which at six months are nearly adult size. About this time the family begins to disperse, the newly independent kits heading off to hunt on their own.

In mid-July a male arctic fox (above) carries a mouthful of lemmings back to the den site where his six-week-old pups (right) are waiting to be fed.

An arctic fox peers through a large patch of fireweed at sunset.

My friend Paul Ratson showed me these rare calypso orchids in the boreal forest near Churchill.

In the early evening a fox pup greets its father at the edge of the boreal forest.

Above: Rough-legged hawks prefer rocky cliffs for their nests.

Below: Mid-August is the peak rutting season for muskoxen near Cambridge Bay on Victoria Island. The "head-banging" can be heard for miles.

Above: A group of young arctic ground squirrels plays outside one of the many entrances to their burrow.

Below: The Cape Churchill caribou herd comprises more than 3,000 animals.

A SURPRISE VISITOR

On my first trip to photograph walruses in 1996, I traveled by dog team out to the floe edge off Southampton Island, at the top of Hudson Bay. For most of the two weeks we camped at Native Point, the strong wind made it impossible to launch our canoe. Without one, we had no way of reaching the walruses hauled out on the ice floes and islands offshore. "It's just a question of time," my guide Luke Eetuk said, and on that particular trip I ran out of it. Luke later gave me the nickname Anvqisiut (an Inuk name meaning "wind man") because on the three occasions I visited that year, the wind picked up when I arrived and died down when I left.

Several years later, I decided to try my luck again, but this time with Brad Parker, an outfitter based in Igloolik, a small community on an island between Nunavut's Melville Peninsula and the northwest coast of Baffin Island. Like Luke, Brad told me that if I had the patience and the time I would get my walrus images. "We can't go out on the water when the wind speed is more than 12 miles (20 kilometers) an hour or when it's foggy or snowing," he explained. "The spray will freeze on the boat, icing it up and making it too heavy. That's why we can only go out in perfect weather conditions."

I waited as patiently as I could, taking advantage of the spare time to photograph the loons, eiders, arctic terns and other migratory birds that arrive in early June to lay their eggs and raise their chicks. Finally, one late afternoon Brad gave the go-ahead. I carried my gear down to the shore to meet Pakak Qamaniq, one of Brad's guides. After negotiating several big pans of ice, our 25-foot-long (7.5-meter) motorboat chugged across

Foxe Basin, our smooth passage interrupted only once, by the crisscross waves of the current created by the Fury and Hecla Strait to the north.

By midnight the sun had nearly reached the horizon. The light grew softer and the temperature dropped below freezing, causing a thin layer of ice to form on the water's surface. Passing through it sounded like the splintering of thousands of tiny glasses. After hours of staring through my binoculars I was suddenly rewarded by the sight of a brown spot on a piece of ice in the far distance. Twenty minutes later we arrived within camera range of the small floe and one of the most touching scenes I have ever photographed – a mother walrus with her newborn calf.

Walruses are sensitive to the sound of motors, so we cut the boat's engine and paddled slowly on a course parallel with the slowly drifting ice. The mother tended to her baby as Pakak and I quietly shared an experience that we both knew we would never have the privilege of witnessing again.

In August I returned to Igloolik, waited for a calm day, then headed out on the ocean once more with Pakak and another guide, Adam Qanatsiaq. Even with three sets of eyes we didn't spot a piece of ice, let alone a walrus, in hours of searching. At dusk we pitched a tent on an island and, as luck would have it, discovered a herd of walruses hauled out on a tiny neighboring island. Although an intermittent fog made it difficult to see them, I decided to try to take some photos with a long telephoto lens. What I didn't know was that I wasn't the only interested observer.

A mature male polar bear suddenly lumbered out of the water between some nearby boulders. The distance between us was much too

At the end of May, Luke Eetuk and I were on our way to the floe edge in search of walruses when I took these photos of Luke and his dogs.

Right: A walrus cow and her newborn calf in the light of the midnight sun.

Although awkward on land, walruses can move quickly once they are in the water – up to 12 miles (20 kilometers) per hour. Strangely enough, this panic was initiated by the shadow of a flock of snow geese flying overhead.

close for comfort. After shaking himself off, much as a dog does after a dip in the lake, he began walking casually toward me. I yelled – more a pathetic yelp than anything that would strike fear in an animal's heart. He ignored me and kept closing the gap between us. Hadn't he seen or heard me? I wasn't his prey, was I? At 55 yards (50 meters) he began to run, and it briefly crossed my mind that maybe I should do the same, despite all the expert advice to the contrary. I was edging into full-blown panic when

he ran past me and slipped back into the water, without giving me so much as a second glance. Obviously my bony human frame was poor fare compared to the blubbery feast spread out on the neighboring islet.

Once our visitor was swimming across the channel between the islands, it seemed like a good time to take some pictures, but my hands were shaking so badly that it took three tries to change the film. I dropped the first two rolls on the ground.

Walruses eat several thousand shellfish a day, resting on ice floes and islands to digest their meals. In the water they have been known to ram boats when they feel threatened.

Meanwhile the walruses had failed to notice the polar bear's stealthy approach. The waves were too high, the fog was too thick and the wind was in his favor. He reached the island and crept up behind the herd. One walrus saw him and gave the alarm, and 300 bulky bodies waddled surprisingly quickly into the sea. In their panic, all but one reached the safety of the water.

A young walrus had become separated from its mother during the stampede. It wasted precious seconds, unsure of what to do. Before it could escape, the polar bear grabbed the walrus by the head, tossed it into the air and played with it like a cat with a mouse, then killed it and settled down to eat its meal.

The hours of waiting and minutes of heart-pumping fear all turned out to be worth it when I developed the photographs from my summer days with the walruses.

Two cubs hitch a ride on their mother's back while keeping an eye on the strange creatures on the floe.

Adult male walruses weigh about 2,800 pounds (1,300 kilograms), while females tip the scales at about 1,500 pounds (700 kilograms).

On this amazing day I was in a boat photographing a group of walruses when a polar bear family moved onto the ice floe.

On a foggy evening in August, a polar bear emerges from the ocean and sneaks up to a walrus herd. The walruses become aware of him and begin stampeding into the water, while the bear looks for its preferred prey, a walrus calf separated from its mother.

Walruses use their long tusks to ward off bears when necessary, but would rather escape into the water than fight. These sudden stampedes can sometimes severely injure animals in the middle of the group.

Around midnight a fog-bow appears over the Arctic Ocean. Its water droplets are too small to split the light into the colors of a rainbow.

I was photographing this bear and her cubs in Foxe Basin, the northern extension of Hudson Bay, when she suddenly noticed our boat. She went on alert for just a moment before continuing on her way. This is one of my favorite photographs of that summer.

FALL

At the beginning of August the Arctic becomes noticeably quieter as the summer visitors leave and life begins to drain from the land. The first frost sets the berry leaves ablaze and turns the tamarack needles to soft gold. The caribou gather in large herds for their annual migration, as do the flocks of geese, ducks and other migrants heading south for the winter.

As the early snows sweep across the tundra, the polar bear begins its own migration, but not south. A follower of ice and snow, this arctic resident heads north.

MORE CLOSE ENCOUNTERS

As fall approaches, the polar bears of the Hudson Bay–James Bay Lowlands begin following the coastline north in search of an early freeze. They reach the Churchill area by mid-October, where they wait for the ice to form a pathway to their seal-hunting grounds. On some days the tundra reminds me of a sheep meadow in Scotland. Sometimes up to 200 white bears can be seen from the air between Cape Churchill and the town proper, making Churchill the only accessible venue in the world where people can see these magnificent animals up close and in such numbers in the wild.

Each year thousands of tourists from around the world hop aboard custom-made all-terrain buses to make a day trip to the polar bears' tundra playground 9 miles outside of Churchill. Tundra Buggy Tours and Great White Bear Tours also offer hotels on wheels for longer stays. Made up of interconnected vehicles, the rolling hotels – fully equipped with a lounge and sleeping quarters – provide both food and lodging for visitors. On one exceptional Tundra Buggy trip to Cape Churchill in 2004, more than 20 polar bear families milled about on the shoreline where the "hotel" was parked. It must have resembled a zoo, with the humans in the cages and the bears roaming freely.

I'm often asked to recommend the best time to visit Churchill during the bear-watching season, which runs roughly from October 10 through the third week in November. But just as there are no set rules governing the weather in this region, there are none for the bears either. The polar bear season relies on the timing of ice freeze up and on the travel schedule of the bears as they make their way up the coast. There may be no bears in early October or they may have left long before early November; just as unpredictably, the season may extend well into December. Regardless of the migration pattern in any one year, all the tour organizers stop offering trips to the tundra by the end of November.

To see these powerful animals up close from a safe vantage point is the experience of a lifetime. But there is a difference between up close and too close. Most bears have their own agendas that have nothing to do with humans. On occasion, though, while working in the field I have found myself in alarming proximity to a curious or hungry animal.

One year I was parked in a truck observing a gang of seven bears that had been milling about for several hours – not an unusual circumstance in the fall. An older bear slowly approached the vehicle, circled it and then stood up on its hind legs looking for food on the truck bed. Finding nothing edible, the creature settled for mischief instead, moving forward to the front of the truck, where it dropped out of sight behind the hood. Suddenly the truck began to rock back and forth – my white-coated friend was at one of the front wheels, tugging with all its might. Before I could start the engine to scare the bear off it had chomped the tire flat. In a bit of a panic, I wrenched the key in the ignition, jammed the truck into gear and pulled away as fast as I could, thumping overland on the flat tire. I barely made it to the main road, where I was able to put on the spare.

Years later Elli and I stayed at a remote research camp outside Churchill. While we were cooking dinner in the cabin one evening, I spotted a half-grown male bear playing in a nearby lake. He sniffed the air, caught the scent of our food and clambered out of the water. As I watched through the binoculars he started walking toward us through the bushes and a little swamp, picking up speed as he drew closer and the smell grew stronger.

Once he reached the tall wire fence surrounding the compound, it was obvious that he had decided nothing, including the fence, was going to prevent him from eating our dinner. He bit, shoved and pulled at the wire mesh. When that didn't work, he rose up on his hind legs and started pushing against the wooden fence posts until they began creaking ominously. Soon our uninvited dinner guest was running around outside the fence searching for a weak spot and getting more frustrated by the minute.

Elli and I put every bear deterrent method we knew into practice. First we yelled and banged pot lids together. The bear simply lowered his head and growled. Then I picked up the shotgun and fired cracker shells into the air. He became even angrier. Finally, after a half-hour standoff, I radioed for help. While we waited the 30 minutes it would take for the helicopter to pick us up, the camp manager recommended using pepper spray. After testing the wind direction, I walked up to the piece of fence the bear was busy trying to dismantle and sprayed him in the face. Roaring with anger, he raced to the lake to wash the stuff out of his eyes. By the time the helicopter was lifting off to take us back to town, our juvenile delinquent, undeterred, was heading back to the camp.

The next day we flew back over the research camp. The bear was resting in some willows nearby. Although it was disappointing, I gave up on the idea of photographing in the area. With this bear nearby, walking around on the tundra, even with a local hunter watching my back, was not an option, and I didn't want to be responsible for shooting a hungry bear in self-defense. I later learned that this particular bear had a broken tooth, which must have been extremely painful.

Studies have shown that the risk of being killed by a polar bear in the Far North is far smaller than the risk of being struck by lightning, dying from a bee sting or being killed in a train crash. A University of Calgary study examined 381 incidents involving bears and humans between 1965 and 1985 and found that 353 of them caused no harm and 28 involved injury; in eight cases the injuries were deadly. Bears are not wanton man-eaters – in each of these cases the people were carrying food, making them prime targets for a hungry bear.

From the burgeoning ecotourism industry to geological surveys and resource extraction, human activities have placed people in close proximity to polar bears, thus bringing about an increase in bear–human contact. It is important to keep in mind who the interloper is in the Arctic, and to act accordingly.

Our uninvited dinner guest leans against the fence surrounding the research camp.

Above: For approximately two weeks, thousands of snow geese migrate through the Hudson Bay–James Bay Lowlands, stopping to feed and to wait for the right wind to carry them south. Huge flocks feeding on the hillsides look like an avalanche when they move.

Left: In this aerial view of Wapusk National Park, the first snow has fallen but the lakes are not yet frozen.

A red fox (above) and an arctic hare (below) yawn after a nap.

Above: A hungry arctic fox tries and fails to catch a Canada goose.

Below: Two male muskoxen rest during the first blizzard of the fall.

Above: Black spruce lean away from the prevailing northwest wind on an early November evening.

Left: In the fall the red leaves of alpine bearberry and blueberry carpet many parts of the Hudson Bay–James Bay Lowlands.

Above: While waiting for the ice to form on Hudson Bay, this bear found a discarded tire on the tundra and began to play with it.

Right: As one bear takes a look at the beginning of a play-fight, another prepares to take a snooze.

One year several orphaned cubs appeared outside Churchill. This one was sleeping in a snowbank, woke up and yawned into the camera. The next day it was gone, fate unknown.

WAITING FOR THE ICE TO FORM *Chapter Eight*

On the tundra when the winds are light, the sky gray and the temperatures moderate, the bears are not very active. However, when a cold wind blows in from the north, the sun shines and slush begins forming on the bay, the bears become as excited as the tourists watching them – milling about, venturing out on the ice to test its thickness and wrestling with one another.

Polar bears are the largest terrestrial carnivore in the world, so it is not surprising that the mock fights of the young males at Churchill never fail to impress, even though they won't reach their maximum size until they are about 10 years of age. Standing erect on hind legs, the white giants often engage in hours of good-natured wrestling, taking turns biting an opponent's ears and neck, then dragging him to the ground. The bears tumble about on the snow like a pair of well-choreographed Hollywood stunt men, shaking fresh powder off their thick coats in long streams of glistening crystals. Just as quickly they'll bounce to their feet and start a shoving match or a fistfight.

It is not unusual to see one panting bear, weary from a confrontation, licking snow to quench his thirst, while his opponent lies spread-eagled on the ice, cooling his stomach. Recovering quickly, each launches a fresh attack, and the bout begins anew. For juveniles such encounters help hone the skills necessary to survive the battles they will face later in life for mates, territory and food. For adults that already know their way around, however, the meaning of these extended play sessions between individuals that will become deadly rivals during breeding season remains a matter of speculation. Some scientists suggest that play may be purely circumstantial – a kind of when-in-Rome philosophy – while others argue that play may give even the most experienced bears an opportunity to assess the competition long before any real fight, when the stakes are much higher.

One morning before sunrise, I returned to the spot where I had last seen my polar pugilists of the day before. The sky, which had cleared overnight, was turning bright red as I noticed the duo lying peacefully on the ice. Spent from a recent bout, they were eating generous helpings of snow to cool down as the fiery sun peeked over the horizon. Moments later the bears rose to their feet and began flailing outstretched forelegs, aiming to land a decisive blow. But soon, after a few lackluster jabs, each retreated to a favorite snowdrift and flopped down for a well-earned rest.

For the polar bear families this time of waiting for the ice to form is not all fun and games. Mothers must still protect their yearlings from male bears. The family remains together for one-and-a-half to two years (up to two-and-a-half years in the more northerly regions), with the cubs nursing throughout this period while they learn how to hunt. When they do leave their mothers, juvenile polar bears often travel together, like roving bands of teenagers, until they are mature enough to start their own families.

Polar bears on land spend much of their time resting and conserving energy.

Two polar bears and a raven watch a wolf pass by outside Churchill.

Above: If another male comes too close without an invitation, a roar combined with a threatening lunge is enough to drive the intruder away.

Below: A female (note the radio-collar) protects her cub from a much larger male.

Above: Before the bears return to the sea ice, food shortages can reduce even the most powerful to hunting for mice.

Left: A bear stretches after a long nap.

Above: Cape Churchill is an excellent place to see mothers and cubs. The mothers are on the alert all the time.

This mother
sniffs the air
for potential
threats.

Powder snow had been falling all day long. When these two males started play-fighting, a light wind had come up. I moved into a position where the low evening sun was behind them. I could hear the bears' heavy breathing, their paws swishing through the air and their jaws snapping. I was shooting so fast that Elli had problems loading and reloading the second and third camera bodies fast enough to keep up!

LEAVING THE LAND

The most beautiful landscapes are found in the most unexpected places. In mid-September of 2003, I flew east in a helicopter along the Hudson Bay shoreline of Wapusk National Park. At 1,000 feet the lowlands appeared to be striped with narrow bands of shore and sandbank, followed by broader bands of esker and muskeg. Far to the west the first line of spruce trees marked the edge of the boreal forest. We passed over the snakelike Broad River carrying its immense load of sediment. Farther south the Owl River drains into the bay as well. And it was here, as we flew over its delta, that I caught my breath in surprise. The channels of the river mouth merged with the sea to form one of the most incredible landscapes I had ever seen.

In mid-October I flew over the same route again. All the vivid colors of the previous month had disappeared. The wind had pushed the freshly formed ice to one side of the lakes and ponds, making them look like half-closed eyes. Two weeks later they were frozen, and slush had built up all along the coast. The transformation of the bay had begun.

South of Cape Churchill 15 bears relaxed in their gravel "beds" right next to each other, snacking on the seaweed growing nearby. From their perch on the shoreline, they could watch the ice forming.

The bears choose this area for their seasonal migration onto the ice for a very good reason. The geographic layout of the coast in the Churchill area and the region's tides, winds, currents and temperatures combine to speed up the ice-forming process. Running almost straight north and south, the coastline makes a sharp bend to the east at Churchill, where a landmass protrudes into the bay and forms the upturned hook of Cape Churchill. In October strong winds push new ice forming up north along the coast in a southerly direction, where it quickly accumulates – along with locally forming young ice – in the shallow water off the Cape.

The cycle isn't complete, however, until the open waters of Hudson Bay freeze over, a process that can take from two days (as was the case in 1991) to two weeks. By late October or early November strong winds from the north have driven air temperatures down to –4° F (–20° C). This flash-freezing is accompanied by high winds (35–50 mph/55–80 kph) that blow heavy snow across the water and send icy 12-foot waves crashing onto the rocky shore. As crystals form, the bay's surface is transformed into a heavy slush. Once the temperature drops below –4° F (–20° C), the retreating tide deposits the first solid crust of ice along the coast. The motion of the incoming tide, like a hydraulic compactor, forces any young ice inland, where it forms a solid foundation that becomes the most sought-after new habitat for hungry bears.

Within a few nights of this dramatic metamorphosis, Hudson Bay has assumed its winter mantle – an uninterrupted white vista stretching to the horizon. As I looked through my binoculars, this time from land, I could just make out several cream-colored dots in the distance. The polar bears were leaving the land once more.

Above: An aerial view of the slushy surface of Hudson Bay on a late November evening, just before the bay froze over.

Right: The colorful patterns in this aerial photograph of the Owl River delta are created by runoff channels, sandbanks above and below the water's surface, and sediment entering Hudson Bay.

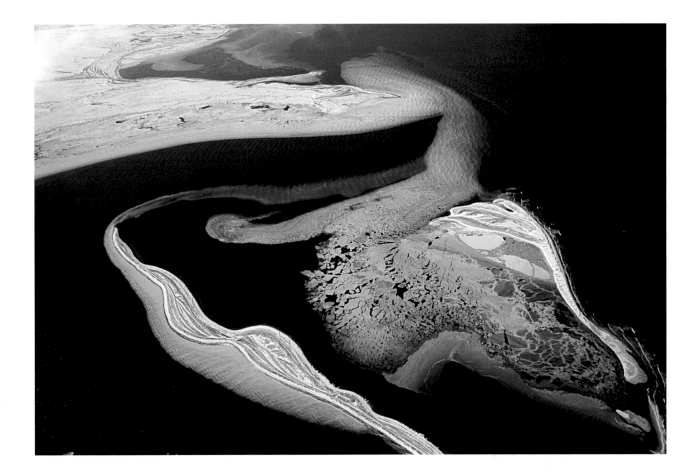

Above: Keyask Island.

Below: Recently frozen lakes and a huge esker in Wapusk National Park.

Left: The Broad River flows through marshland and eskers before draining into large tidal flats along Hudson Bay.

Above: Along the Cape Churchill shoreline, bears bed down in the kelp next to the waterline. They are ready to leave the land as soon as the ice is strong enough to carry their weight.

Right: Far out on the drifting sea ice, a mother and twins settle down after being chased by two male bears.

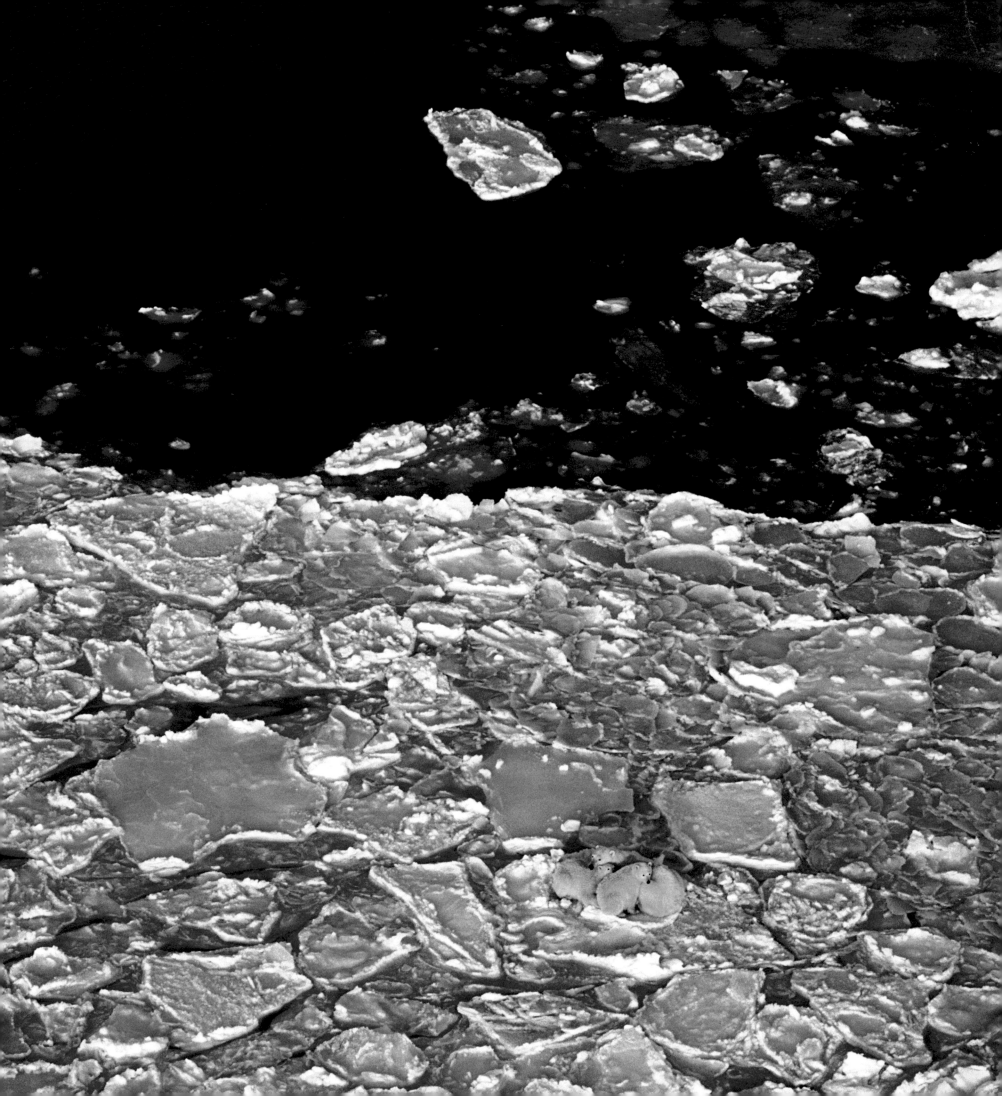

WINTER

*S*now sometimes falls gently in the Arctic. But usually it slashes and whips sideways across the tundra, driven by powerful winds. Surprisingly, over the long, dark winter the region receives less snow than many places farther south, the difference being that it remains on the ground for many months, becoming wind-hardened in the process.

Below the concrete-hard top layer of snow, voles and lemmings scurry about in an underground world of tunnels and storage areas. Muskoxen use their massive heads to break the crust in search of the vegetation below. Ptarmigan seek shelter beneath the drifts. Only the ravens, arctic foxes and polar bears seem to genuinely enjoy this season as they crisscross the sea ice. For this trio of species, winter is the most bountiful time of the year.

ADAPTING TO THE ARCTIC

While its southern cousins are snoozing the late winter away, the polar bear is at the peak of its activity – with the exception of pregnant females, which must set up dens to prepare for the birth of their cubs. Thanks to its carnivorous disposition, the polar bear spends the winter roaming about on the vast ice pack in search of a steady supply of high-protein meals.

Modern bears, which are the largest of the terrestrial carnivores, have evolved into eight species worldwide: brown, American black, polar, sun, sloth, panda, Asiatic black and spectacled. The last descendant to appear in this long evolutionary line was the polar bear. Piecing together the history of the species from fossilized records, researchers believe that the polar bear came into existence roughly 100,000 years ago, a descendant of brown bears from Siberia that had become stranded in the Arctic by advancing glaciation. (Theories about the close relationship between these two species are supported by the fact that they can crossbreed when in captivity.) Cold though the new habitat may have been, an abundance of high-fat seals and the absence of competition and predation made the transformation possible.

Shaped by thousands of years of natural history, the polar bear is an arctic specialist, uniquely adapted to survive in the perpetually challenging environment of the Far North. Acute senses and agility further distinguish the polar bear's survival skills on the arctic terrain. Its sense of smell is phenomenal: It can detect young seals hiding in a snow cave buried under 3 feet (1 meter) of snow nearly a mile (1.6 kilometers) away. Its vision, which tends to be farsighted, allows the bear to scan the endless landscape, while its hearing is comparable to that of humans.

Good insulation provides the first line of defense against the cold, and *Ursus maritimus* wears a warm "coat" of three layers: dense fur (guard hairs and a thick underwool that traps heat), skin and fat. When densely packed together, these hairs form a coat in a range of vanilla, creamy and pale yellow hues. Adding up to 4 inches (10 centimeters) of cold-fighting protection, its coat amply protects the polar bear from fierce blizzards and the icy polar waters in which it swims. Its hollow guard hairs and fat also help keep the bear buoyant in the water – a particularly useful feature, given that scientists recently tracked a tagged bear that swam at least 46 miles (74 kilometers) in just one day.

Evidence of the polar bear's efficient insulation came to light unexpectedly when a scientist was attempting to take aerial photographs of suspected bear habitats using infrared film. Infrared film is highly sensitive to thermal radiation and is therefore an almost foolproof way to document the movements of warm-blooded animals. Yet the only sign of bears the photographs showed was the thermal imaging of their breath. While the results were disappointing for the polar bear census takers, this exercise inadvertently demonstrated that the hardy carnivore is remarkably well insulated, radiating almost none of its precious body heat.

A polar bear's foot pads are not only rough enough to provide traction but are also thickly furred and immune to frostbite, while its small ears are threaded with a fine network of blood vessels that transport sufficient thermal energy to the exposed auricles to keep them from freezing. From the soles of its feet to the tips of its ears, the polar bear has evolved to cope with the cold.

Like other northern animals and birds, polar bears allow the snow to drift around them to provide insulation.

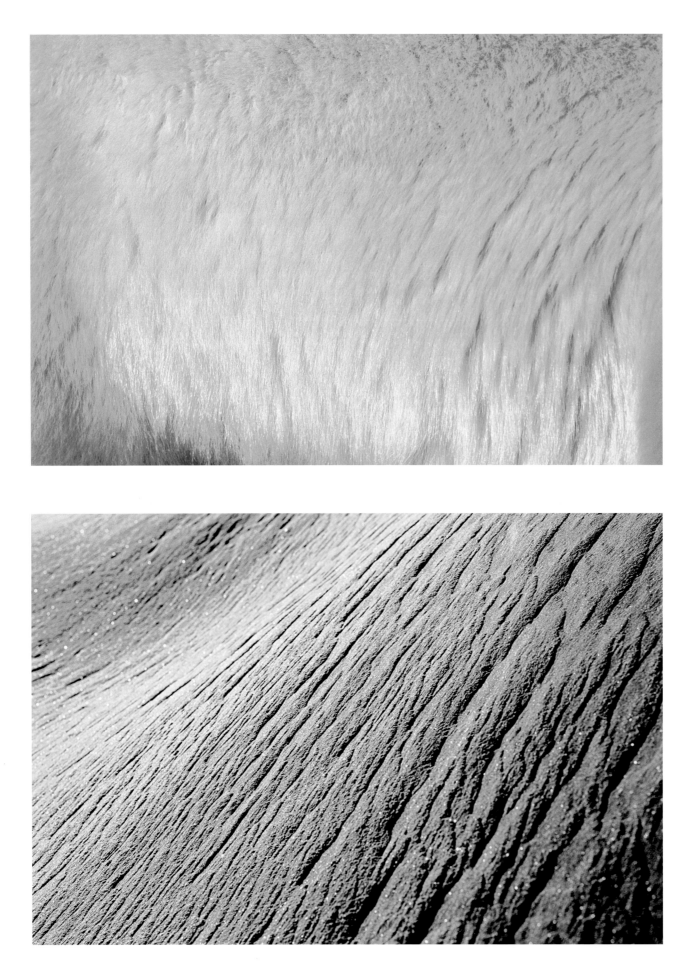

Close-ups of polar bear fur (above) and a snowdrift in the morning light (below).

Right: With its long claws a polar bear can pull a 600-pound (270 kg) seal out of its breathing hole.

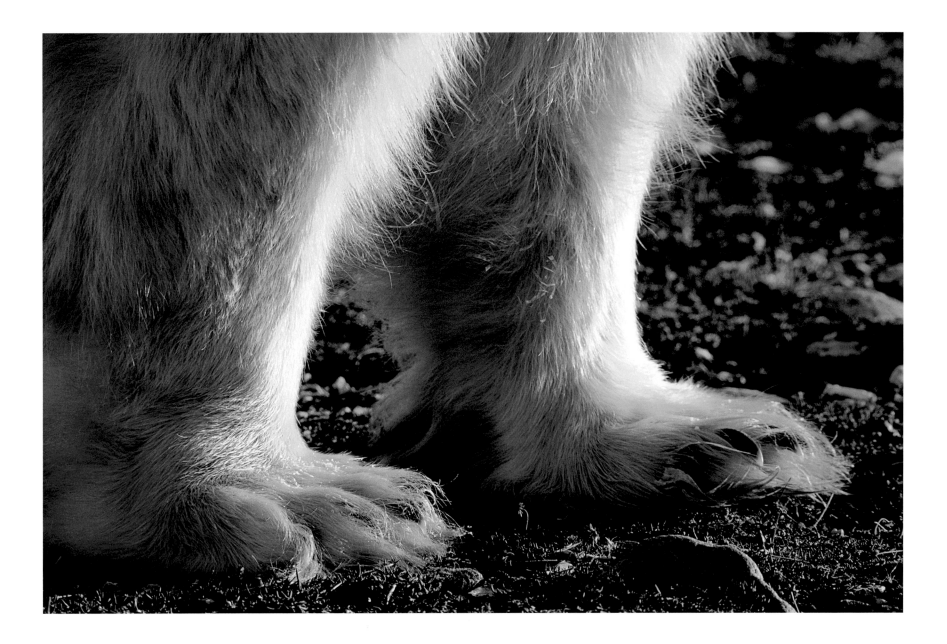

Right: The ice on the Churchill River moves and cracks with the tides. An arctic fox crosses the frozen river.

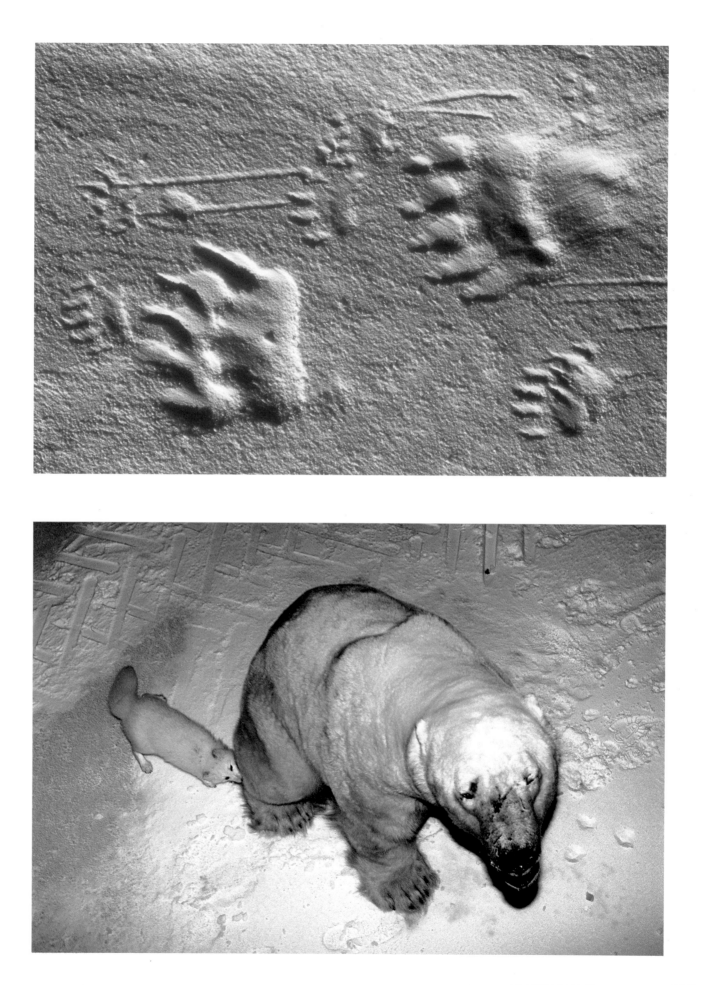

Above: Footprints of a female polar bear and her three-month-old cub.

Below: A fox bites a bear, perhaps to urge it to go hunting (page 162).

Like arctic foxes, ravens sometimes follow polar bears out onto the ice to scavenge on seals. The northern raven lives year-round in the Churchill area, one of the few birds able to survive the long arctic winter.

This bear was sleeping in a snowbank. We wouldn't have seen him at all if he hadn't poked his head up just as we were passing by. He began to do his morning exercises, stretching his muscles to get ready for another day in the cold. He worked out for quite a while, not seeming to mind the amused spectators.

Polar bears rarely catch and kill red foxes, which may be why this one is walking by the bear so calmly.

SKY PHENOMENA

I've always thought it was fitting that the land of the polar bear derives its name from *arktos*, the Greek word for bear. The constellations dominating the night sky of the Arctic, Ursa Major and Ursa Minor (the Latin words for great bear and little bear), first suggested the name. In the absence of the light pollution that hides stars from city dwellers in the south, the night skies of the Arctic are indeed a stargazer's dream. Even more breathtaking, though, are the region's famous optical phenomena.

One clear January morning I drove out of Churchill after breakfast and noticed an immense wall of fog building up over the ice of Hudson Bay. High tides and heavy ocean currents had cracked the pack ice in places, revealing the dark water below. The temperature difference between the –35° F (–37° C) air and the relatively warm water had produced the fog, which a light breeze from the northeast was blowing over the land. As vapor rises from these stretches of open water, the water droplets freeze and become ice crystals. Billions of these ice-fog crystals reflect the light, creating wonderful optical effects.

As with every photographic subject in the Arctic, one can be lucky and see these phenomena nearly every day or unlucky and wait for weeks to witness one. This particular morning I was lucky. The entire sky was filled with sundogs, halos and arcs, almost too many for even a wide-angle lens to record. That night I observed the same effect around the moon.

Although these celestial events are spectacular, the Arctic is probably best known for another sky phenomenon: the northern lights, or aurora borealis. February, March and April are the best times of the year to observe this otherworldly spectacle, and because Churchill, Yellowknife, NWT, and Fairbanks, Alaska, lie beneath the "auroral oval," they are three of the best places in the world to view the dancing lights.

The northern lights originate with eruptions on the sun. Their visible light and color are created by solar energy particles striking gas particles in the ionosphere, which is between 300 and 620 miles (480 to 1,000 kilometers) above the Earth's surface. A steady stream of these particles, comprising both positive and negative electrical charges, radiates from the sun at approximately 600 miles (965 kilometers) per second, in what is known as the solar wind. After traveling through space for about a day, the charged particles of the solar wind strike the Earth's magnetosphere, accelerating along the lines of the magnetic field toward the geomagnetic poles. At these points the solar particles bombard the Earth's atmosphere, and the nitrogen and oxygen in the atmosphere begin to glow.

When the energy particles strike nitrogen at high altitudes, the northern lights glow blue or purple. Nitrogen at low altitudes appears red. When the particles strike oxygen, the light produced has a greenish hue, except at altitudes above 155 miles (250 kilometers), where the gas glows bright red.

But a scientific explanation cannot equal the wonder of experiencing the northern lights firsthand. Near midnight one bitterly cold night, the sky flickered in the east. A transparent green spot in the distance raced toward me, growing in size. It was dragging a long, sweeping tail whose luminous rays were woven together in a fluttering display. From one second to the next this half-coiled greenish yellow snake filled the sky, and its undulating palette warmed the snowy landscape with a chartreuse glow. The aurora slithered west, releasing strands of light in serpentine spasms. At 1:30 a.m., the molten-orange moon peeked above the horizon and another auroral wave billowed across the sky. Occasionally, like diaphanous curtains, the sheets of light parted and released an illuminated dust. Then they passed slowly in front of the glorious moon, fading as they traveled west.

Then suddenly, the aurora erupted straight overhead, in bright red and purple needles that clustered in colorful bundles. The light beams surrounded me, and I felt as if I were in the middle of a spinning carousel. The "symphony of eternity," as Norwegian polar explorer Fridtjof Nansen called it, danced about me, its rays and beams giving off green, amber, purple and red light. At that moment I recalled the Spartan eloquence of polar explorer Robert Scott as he described his first encounter with this celestial event: "It is impossible to view these phenomena without standing in awe."

Above: A long green aurora moves noiselessly across the sky at dusk.

Left: In mid-September, as the moon rises over Schmok Lake near the Nunavut–Manitoba border, an aurora glows in the sky.

Sundogs, a halo and an arc appear over the tree line on a cold December day. Drifting and falling ice crystals create these unusual phenomena.

Northerners enjoy spectacular sunsets. Ice crystals in the high atmosphere created these flame-like skies near Churchill.

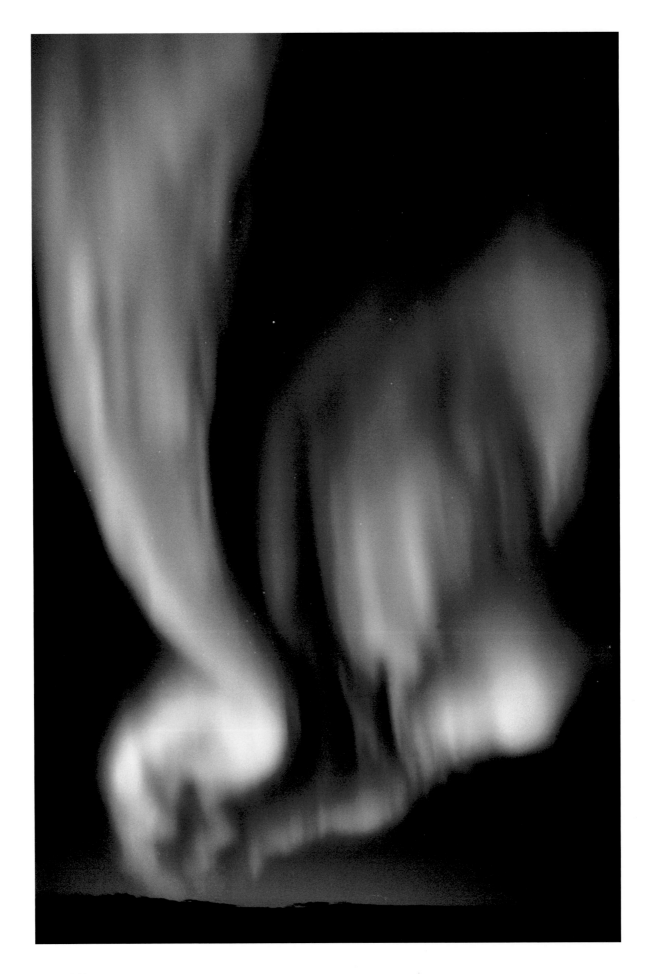

The northern lights, photographed with a fisheye lens outside an igloo (above) and at dusk (left).

This photograph of the aurora and a full moon was taken on a clear, very cold winter night.

Following page: I had just a brief moment to take this photo of an arctic fox on a bitterly cold morning in February. Within minutes the fox ran off and the camera died.

A HABITAT OF ICE AND SNOW

Chapter Twelve

For three days one February a snowstorm raged through Churchill, paralyzing the town. With peak gales reaching 48 miles (77 kilometers) per hour and outside temperatures sinking to –22° F (–30° C), the local television station issued a warning that the wind-chill factor was the ambient equivalent of about –90° F (–68° C).

Every step outside on such bone-chilling days produces aches and pains that are only exaggerated by the futility of trying to move about in the raging whiteout. There is no point of reference to help keep you oriented – landmarks such as buildings and cars are visible for mere seconds in the frosty vortex.

By early morning, however, the world was transformed. The storm had died down, and the sun, low on the horizon, washed the snow-blown landscape in a palette of warm tones. As the sky overhead brightened, thousands of glistening snowflakes filled the air. They clung to the remnants of summer grasses and settled in artistic shapes on the lee side of rocks, trees and houses. No sculptor could have been more imaginative.

Viewing a meringue-like drift from an angle, I could see ice crystals blowing across the upper edge and falling gently, like powdered sugar, to form a new shape below. Such endless sifting of windswept crystals creates huge white walls. Originally hexagonal snowflakes, these crystals have been blown across the tundra until collisions with rocks, trees and branches have shattered their original symmetry, reducing them to

tiny ice needles a millimeter or less in length. Pressure from the mighty northern wind then packs the crystals into dense drifts of unexpected structural stability. The density of a typical drift measures about 25 pounds per cubic foot (400 kilograms per cubic meter). By comparison, freshly fallen snow has a density of about one pound per cubic foot (16 kilograms per cubic meter).

Polar bears have an intimate connection with snow. To clean themselves off after a greasy seal repast in the summer, they go for a bath in the nearest body of water, but in the winter they roll about in the snow. Like most arctic birds and animals, while they rest they allow the snow to drift up around their bodies to provide insulation and shelter from the heat-draining wind. They tuck themselves into as compact a shape as possible, with their hindquarters or side to the wind, to further reduce heat loss. When the weather turns particularly frigid or stormy, the bears hollow out temporary shelters in snowdrifts. And, of course, most cubs enter the world surrounded by the encompassing snow of their maternity den.

Over the years that I have been photographing these magnificent animals, I have grown to respect their ability to survive in the ice and snow of the Far North. It is devastating to think that the polar bear's habitat may be endangered by global warming. They deserve much better from us.

Above: Strong winds whip up ice crystals and continuously change the shapes of snowdrifts in Wapusk National Park.

The boreal forest in early March.

A snow sculpture created by the wind on the lee side of a hill.

AFTERWORD

The polar bear is one of the most recognized symbols of the Arctic and is of tremendous cultural and spiritual importance to the aboriginal peoples who live there. Distributed among 19 populations, the total number of polar bears throughout the world is thought to be 20,000–25,000. Superbly adapted to their surroundings, they have evolved to become specialized predators of ice-breeding seals. A significant adaptation that has enabled polar bears to exploit and thrive in the seemingly unforgiving and unpredictable arctic environment is their ability to slow down their metabolism at any time of the year to conserve energy when seals are scarce. In areas where the sea ice melts completely each summer, polar bears are able to spend several months on land by fasting and living off stored fat reserves. Nowhere is this more remarkable than in the southern extremes of their range, such as Hudson Bay, where bears of most age and sex classes fast for four months, and pregnant females do so for up to eight months.

Historically, the greatest potential threat to polar bears has been over-harvesting. Fortunately polar bears are one of the better-managed species. Growing concern about the increasing numbers of polar bears being harvested in the 1950s and 1960s led to the formation of the IUCN Polar Bear Specialist Group in 1968 and negotiation of an international Agreement on the Conservation of Polar Bears and Their Habitat (1973), which was unanimously ratified by all five "polar bear countries" (Canada, Denmark, Norway, the United States and the Union of Soviet Socialist Republics). The future of the polar bear appeared secure.

However, despite these and other important conservation initiatives that have helped maintain healthy polar bear populations throughout much of their historical range, large-scale ecological change in the Arctic's environment poses a significant threat to the future welfare of polar bears. For example, the annual breakup of sea ice on western Hudson Bay is now occurring three weeks earlier than it did in the early 1970s. Polar bears have less time on the sea ice and fewer hunting opportunities to build fat reserves before coming ashore. In addition,

bears have to fast for longer on these diminished resources. Ongoing research of the western Hudson Bay population has shown that bears are not coming ashore as fat as they used to, that most mothers are keeping their cubs an additional year before weaning, and that changes in cub production and survival have occurred. However, because polar bears are long-lived and rely on high rates of adult survival to offset the impact of living in an unpredictable environment, poor cub production and survival in any one year have little long-term effect on the population as long as environmental conditions improve and adults survive to reproduce another year.

This appeared to be the case in western Hudson Bay, where, despite the earlier breakup of sea ice and lost hunting opportunities, the population remained stable near 1,200 individuals through the mid-1990s. Unfortunately, polar bear life history cannot counter the cumulative and ongoing negative effects of a warming climate. Of greatest concern is that the size of the western Hudson Bay population has declined to fewer than 950 polar bears within the past decade. While some may question and debate what has caused the climate to change, the projections agree that much of the Arctic will continue to warm. Furthermore, there are suggestions that the multiyear sea ice cover may disappear, or at least be substantially reduced, within a hundred years. Should the current trends continue and the projections prove to be reasonably accurate, then the future of the polar bear looks very bleak. The world would almost certainly lose the southernmost populations of polar bears, such as those of western Hudson Bay.

It is tragic that we are in very real danger of losing such a magnificent and powerful animal, one that has evolved to be the ultimate arctic predator. As I look back on the past 25 years of my life, I feel very fortunate to have had the opportunity to spend my research career in polar regions. I look into the future with great sadness, and wonder what legacy we are leaving those that follow.

– Nick Lunn, Research Scientist, Canadian Wildlife Service

ON WILDLIFE PHOTOGRAPHY

Only a few places on Earth offer as rich a diversity of scenes that can be "painted" with a camera as does the Arctic. Setting aside the challenges of the climate – having to handle equipment at –22° F (–30° C), for instance – late fall, winter and early spring offer dramatic opportunities for capturing the soft, dreamlike texture of reddish-tinged light. Gradual changes in the light's intensity and color from horizon to horizon add a certain mystique to this part of the world.

Standing in the middle of the northern night with its myriad stars above, I am always awestruck at the magic of the aurora borealis caressing the velvety dark skies. Like a giant orange ball, the full moon rises above the horizon with an exceptional purity and beauty. While a painter might reach for a palette and brush, incorporating his own imagination, I must engrave these miracles on a piece of thin plastic.

I find that my education never ends, and I am constantly pushing myself to learn more. Familiarity with your equipment and its idiosyncrasies is essential, as is training your visual perception and imagination, extensive study of your subject matter and an ever-broadening knowledge of photographic techniques, which comes from reading books and magazines, visiting art and photography exhibits and sharing information with other photographers and nature lovers.

Just before I press the shutter-release button, I concentrate solely on the image in the viewfinder. Closing my ears to surrounding noises, such as chattering birds or the wind, I ask myself these questions: What is the message of the picture before my eyes? Will the casual observer understand what I am seeing at this very moment? Dedicated consideration of such questions is the key to creating good photographs and has helped me become an inspired and satisfied "painter with a camera."

Following the introduction of the R6, I switched to the Leica R system in 1989. I needed a camera system that could handle the challenges of the harsh arctic environment. Light conditions can be extremely difficult, and I have faced them all: white subjects on a white background, excessive backlight and glare, and long, deep shadows. The optical and mechanical features of the lenses are of the utmost importance in resolving such problems.

Despite the pressure to use digital equipment, I still use the Leica R camera system. I like the fact that my original slide images have not been "touched up" with the click of a mouse.

TECHNICAL INFORMATION

All images in this book were taken with Leica R-System analog (film) cameras. I used the R6.2, R7, R8 and R9 camera bodies and the following Leica lenses: 2.8/16 Fisheye Elmarit, 3.5/15 Super Elmar, 2.8/19 Elmarit, 4.0/21 Super Angulon, 2.8/28 PC Super Angulon, 1.4/35 Summilux, 1.4/50 Summilux, 2.0/50 Summicron, 1.4/80 Summilux, 2.0/90 Summicron, 2.8/100 Apo Makro Elmarit, 2.0/180 Apo Summicron, 2.8/180 Elmarit, 4.0/280 Apo Telyt, 2.8/280 + 2.8/400 + 4.0/560 + 5.6/800 Apo Telyt Module System. Vario (Zoom) lenses: 3.5-4.5/21-35 Vario Elmarit, 2.8-4.5/28-90 Vario Elmarit, 2.8/70-180 Vario Apo Elmarit, 1.4 Apo Extender, Leica Ultravid 10x42 binoculars. Film: Fujichrome Velvia 50, Fujichrome Velvia 100, Fujichrome Provia 400, Kodak Ektachrome VS100.

I also use the Gyro Stabilizer from Ken-Lab, Manfrotto MVB 350 tripod, Linhof Professional tripod, Novoflex ballheads, Novoflex Magic Studio and the Novoflex Flash Art System.

PAGE	CAMERA	LENS	PAGE	CAMERA	LENS	PAGE	CAMERA	LENS
Front cover	R8	5.6/800	71	R8	2.8/180	130	R8	2.8/400
1	R6.2	2.8/100 Makro	72/73	R9	4.0/560	132	R8	4.0/560
2/3	R8	4.0/560	74	R6.2	2.8/280	133/134	R8	5.6/800
4/5	R9	4.0/560		R6.2	4.0/560	135	R8	4.0/560
6/7	R9	4.0/280	75	R6.2	2.8/400	136	R6.2	2.0/50
8	R7	4.0/560	76	R7	4.0/280	137	R6.2	3.4/180
9	R9	5.6/800	78	R7	2.8/100 Makro	138	R8	4.0/560
11	R7	2.8/400	79	R7	1.4/35	139	R8	2.8/400
13	R7	2.8/400	80	R7	4.0/560		R8	5.6/800
15	R9	4.0/560	81	R7	2.8/180	140/141	R9	5.6/800
16/17	R7	2.8/280		R8	4.0/560	142	R8	4.0/560
19	R7	2.0/180	82	R9	4.0/21	144	R9	2.0/90
20	R8	4.0/560	83	R9	2.8/100 Makro + Elpro	145	R9	2.0/90
22	R7	5.6/800 + 1.4 Ext.	84	R9	2.8/100 Makro	146	R9	3.5-4.0/21-35
24	R9	2.8/16 Fisheye		R9	2.8/100 Makro + Elpro + Bellow	147	R9	2.8/70-180
25	R9	2.8/28 PC					R9	3.5/15
26	R9	5.6/800 + 1.4 Ext.	85	R9	2.8/180	148	R9	2.8/180
27	R9	5.6/800	86	R9	4.0/560	149	R9	4.0/280
28	R9	4.0/560	88	Canon EOS 1V	4.0/500 IS	150/151	R9	2.0/180
29	R8	5.6/800	89	R9	2.8/400	153	R9	4.0/280
	R8	4.0/560	90/91	R9	2.8/180 fill-in-flash	154	R9	3.5/15
30	R9	5.6/800	92	R9	2.8/100 Makro	156	R9	2.8/400
31	R8	4.0/560	93	R8	2.8/400	158	R8	4.0/560
32/33	R9	4.0/560	94	R6.2	2.8/400	159	R8	5.6/800
34	R8	4.0/560		R8	4.0/560	160	R9	4.0/560
36-39	R9	5.6/800	95	R7	2.8/280		R9	2.0/180
40	R7	2.8/400		R7	2.0/50	161	R9	2.8/400
41	R7	4.0/560	96	R8	2.0/180	162	R7	4.0/560
	R9	2.8/400	98	R7	2.8/19	163/164	R9	1.4/35
42	R6.2	1.4/35		R7	1.4/35	165	R9	1.4/50
43	R6.2	2.8/100 Makro	99	R8	4.0/280		R8	1.4/50
44	R8	2.8/70-180	100	R8	2.0/180	166	R9	2.8/400
45	R9	5.6/800	101	R8	70-180	167	R8	4.0/280
46/47	R8	2.8/400	102	R8	70-180	168/169	R7	2.8/400
48/49	R6.2	2.8/19	103/104	R8	5.6/800	170/171	R9	4.0/560
50	R7	2.8/100 Makro	105	R8	4.0/280	172	R9	1.4/35
51	R7	2.0/180	106/107	R8	5.6/800	174	R9	1.4/50
52	R8	1.4/50	108/109	R8	2.8/19	175	R9	1.4/50
54	R8	2.8/19	110/111	R8	2.8/70-180	176	R9	3.5/15
55	R8	2.8/28 PC	113	R9	2.8/100 Makro	177	R9	2.8/28 PC
56	R7	4.0/560	114	R9	2.0/90	178	R9	4.0/560
57	R7	4.0/560	116	R9	4.0/280	179	R7	2.0/50
	R7	4.0/560	119	R9	1.4/35	180	R9	1.4/35
59	R9	2.8/100 Makro	120	R9	2.0/90	181	R9	2.8/16 Fisheye
60	R7	1.4/80	121	R9	4.0/560	182/183	R9	2.8/16 Fisheye
62	R8	2.0/180	122	R9	2.0/180	184/185	R8	2.8/100 Makro
64	R6.2	2.8/100 Makro		R9	2.8/400	186	R8	2.8/28 PC
65	R6.2	2.0/50	123	R9	4.0/280	188	R9	3.5/15
	R7	2.8/19		R8	5.6/800	189	R9	2.8/28 PC
66	R7	2.0/180	124	R9	3.5/15	190/191	R6.2	3.5/15
67	R7	1.4/35		R9	4.0/21 with Flash Art	192	R9	5.6/800 + 1.4 Ext.
68	R7	2.8/70-180	125	R8	5.6/800	194/195	R8	2.8/28 PC
	R7	2.8/70-180	126	R6.2	2.8/280	204	R8	2.8/400
69	R7	1.4/35	127	R9	4.0/560			
70	Underwater housing from National Geographic		128/129	R9	4.0/280			

POLAR BEAR FACTS AND FIGURES

SCIENTIFIC NAMES

Polar bears belong to the order Carnivora. Ursidae, the family name of all bears, is broken down into three subfamilies. Ursinae includes polar, brown, sloth and sun bears; the two other subfamilies cover spectacled bears and giant pandas.

POPULATION

+ Estimates of the number of polar bears in the world today range between 20,000–25,000. Government regulation of hunting has more than doubled the population since the 1960s. The species is not generally recognized as endangered.

+ Adult females in the wild live into their late 20s; adult males in the wild live into their late teens or early 20s. The oldest known member of the species lived to be 41 in a zoological park.

PHYSICAL CHARACTERISTICS

+ Males bears, known as boars, usually weigh 770 to 1,400 pounds (350 to 650 kilograms). This is more than twice the size of the average female, which normally weighs 330 to 550 pounds (150 to 250 kilograms).

+ Boars average 8 to 10 feet (2.5 to 3 meters) long; sows are usually much shorter.

+ On polar bears the forelimbs are shorter than the more powerful hind limbs. Paws are usually 12 inches (30 centimeters) and have non-retractable claws. The sole of the foot features a black dimpled pad to maintain traction on ice.

+ Polar bears have black skin covered with a thick, oily fur coat that insulates their body from the cold.

+ Food is swallowed swiftly, in chunks; the polar bear's 42 teeth are used mainly to shear meat and tear hide.

MOVEMENT

+ Although usually slow and lumbering, polar bears can sprint up to 25 miles (40 kilometers) an hour.

+ Polar bears are exceptional swimmers, able to make their way through frigid waters for hours at a time.

SENSES

+ Polar bears' hearing and sight are as sensitive as those of humans.

+ Their acute sense of smell can detect prey more than 20 miles (32 kilometers) away.

HABITAT

+ Polar bears, or evidence of their presence, have been found nearly as far north as the Pole. More commonly, however, the animals do not venture past latitude 82° north because of lack of food in those regions.

DIET

+ Polar bears subsist largely off ringed and bearded seals. Depending on their location and hunger, they will also eat available land mammals such as reindeer, waterfowl, fish and vegetation, and will scavenge whale carcasses and human refuse.

+ Polar bears use three main methods to catch their prey. Still-hunting involves waiting motionless beside a ledge or breathing hole for a seal to surface. Stalking is used to catch seals sunning themselves on the ice; the polar bear maintains a distance of 50 to 100 feet (15 to 30 meters) before making a sprint to grab the seal. The aquatic stalk is also used to catch seals on the ice; the polar bear will approach by water, then quickly emerge and clamp down on its prey.

REPRODUCTION

+ Polar bears are solitary for the greater part of their lives, although two social units do exist: a mating couple and an adult female with her cubs.

+ By four years of age female polar bears have usually reached sexual maturity. Males often require an additional two years, and many fail to mate successfully until they are eight or ten.

+ Females breed only once every three years, during April and May, causing fierce competition among mature males.

+ Gestation lasts approximately eight months.

+ Cubs are usually born in pairs and weigh about 16 to 24 ounces (450 to 680 grams) each. Blind and deaf for the first few weeks of life, they will be nursed by their mother for up to 30 months.

PACIFIC OCEAN

NORTH
AMERICA

ARCTIC OCEAN

Churchill ●

ASIA

ATLANTIC OCEAN

EUROPE

Polar bear range

Range uncertain, but
bears probably occur
at very low densities

DEDICATION

My thanks to Elli, my wife, mentor and companion. For letting me go whenever I needed to. For following me to remote areas with suitcases full of equipment. For enduring bitterly cold winter nights and melting hot temperatures with me. For being my bear monitor and keeping the tent comfortable. Also, for sharing beautiful times between the tours.

ACKNOWLEDGMENTS

Special thanks to: Gogol Lobmayr for taking me on an unforgettable tour. For friendship: Michael Martin and Elke Wallner, Günter und Sibsi Lenz, Bernd and Manuela Ritschel, John and Anna Echave. My family at home: Ludger, Margret, Elisabeth and Monika, Georg, Elke, Fabian and Leon, Waltraud, Dieter, Charlotte, Bernd and Juergen, Fritz, Annerose, Michael, Irene and Helmut, Dietlind and Hartwig Hagenguth. The entire team of Firefly Books Ltd.

In Churchill:
Brian Ladoon for friendship and support over the years; M&M Ventures: Mike, Lawreen and Morris Spence, Allan Oman (called: Amak), James Spence, Tommy Saunders and Darryl McLaughlin and the entire crew of Wat'chee Lodge; Mike Macri and family from Sea North Tours; Cam Elliott, Bob Reside, Melissa Gibbens, Sarah Boyli and Stacy Jack and the staff of Wapusk National Park; Merv and Lynda Gunter from Tundra Buggy tours; Don and Marylin Walkosky from Great White Bear Tours; Peter (Pete) Anderson; Edgar Botelho; Murry Gillespie; Nick Lunn from the Canadian Wildlife Service; Bonnie Chartier from Churchill Wilderness Encounter; Roger Woloshyn, the Starman; Mike Goodyear and Heather McLeod from the Churchill Northern Study Centre; Claude Daudet from Gyrfalcon Expeditions; Robert and Caroline Buchanan from Polar Bears International; Hudson Bay Helicopters: Tony Bembridge, Joan Brauner and the entire crew, especially the artist in the air: Louis Lemieux; Paul and Matt Ratson from Adventure Walking Tours; The Webber family from Webber's Lodges; Tony, Helen, Frederic, Jessica and Vasco Da Silva from Gypsy's Bakery; Leona Tkachyk, the good soul of Churchill and her excellent cooking and story telling; Mark Ingelbrigston from North Star Tours; The Eskimo Museum; Louise Foubert and Dwight Allen and family from the Polar Inn; Penny and Jenny Rawlings from the Arctic Trading Company; Wayne Bildenduke; Kevin Burke; Calm Air International; Air Canada; Churchill Motel; Seaport Hotel; Betty Brenner from Northern Images; Bill Calnan; and everybody we cannot mention here who ever helped us in Churchill.

In Coral Harbour:
Luke Eetuk, my friend and guide and his family.

In Holman:
Morris Nigijok and his family, Donald Nataina, Allen Pogotak and Harold Wright.

In Cambridge Bay:
Kevin Smart, who opened many door for me up there and who loves the outdoors; Luke Cody, the Laserich family, Joe and Susie, Allen Kitigon and Amos Wamikon.

In Igloolik:
Brad Parker and his family from Igloolik Outdoor Adventures Pakak Qamaniq, Kevin Attaggutaluktuk and Adam Qanatsiaq

Leica Camera AG Germany; Novoflex Praezisionstechnik, Memmingen, Germany.

The Publisher gratefully acknowledges the generous contribution of Moveable Inc. in making this book possible.

BIBLIOGRAPHY

Bastedo, Jamie. *Falling for Snow: A Naturalist's Journey into the World of Winter*. Calgary: Red Deer Press, 2003

Bruemmer, Fred. *World of the Polar Bears*. Toronto: Key Porter Books, 1989

Davis, Neil. *The Aurora Watcher's Handbook*. Fairbanks: University of Alaska Press, 1992

Greenler, Robert. *Rainbows, Halos and Glories*. Cambridge: Cambridge University Press, 1980

Lynch, Wayne. *A is for Arctic: Natural Wonders of a Polar World*. Toronto: Firefly Books, 1996

Ovsyanikov, Nikita. *Polar Bears: Living with the White Bear*. Vancouver: Raincoast Books, 1996

Stirling, Ian. *Polar Bears*. Toronto: Fitzhenry & Whiteside, 1988

WEBSITES

Churchill Northern Studies Centre, www.churchillmb.net/~cnsc/

Great White Bear Tours, www.greatwhitebeartours.com

Hinterland Who's Who, Canadian Wildlife Service, www.hww.ca

Leica, www.leica-camera.com

National Geographic Image Collection, www.ngsimages.com

Norbert Rosing, www.rosing.de

Novoflex, www.novoflex.de

Polar Bears International, www.polarbearsalive.org

Species at Risk, Environment Canada, www.speciesatrisk.gc.ca

Tundra Buggy Adventure, Frontiers North, www.tundrabuggy.com

Wapusk National Park of Canada, www.pc.gc.ca/pn-np/mb/wapusk/

INDEX

Page numbers in *italics* indicate photographs.